THE SOULOLOGY CHRONICLES

VOICES

WORDS OF WISDOM, INSPIRATION, COURAGE AND SOUL

THE SOULOLOGY CHRONICLES

VOICES

WORDS OF WISDOM, INSPIRATION, COURAGE AND SOUL

LISA ANDERSON • NATASHA AZADI • RANJINI CASSUP
JENNIFER CHAPMAN • PATRICIA DE PICCIOTTO
HEATHER DI SANTO • BRI DIMIT • ERIN MONTGOMERY
CASSANDRA NAGEL • FRANCA NAVARRA • CARL RICHARDS
REESHEMAH STIDHUM • MARSHA MYLES TERRY
MARIEKE VAN ASTEN • KAREM ZAFRA-VERA • DELLA WADDELL

Star House
PUBLISHING

For any information regarding permission and bulk purchases contact:

www.starhousepublishing.com or email
info@starhousepublishing.com

ISBN PAPERBACK   978-1-989535-50-9
ISBN HARDCOVER   978-1-989535-51-6
ISBN E-BOOK   978-1-989535-49-3

Printed in the United States of America
First Edition, 2021.

Design by: Susanne Clark | Creative Blueprint Design
Edited by: Jackie Brown

CONTENTS

Step out of the history
that is holding you back.
Step into the new story
you are willing to create.

OPRAH WINFREY

LISA ANDERSON

Lisa Anderson is a published author, certified Master Hypnotist as well as a Reiki Practitioner. She has helped many clients over the years and has become a top Readers Choice Award recipient for hypnotherapists. Lisa currently lives in Ontario, Canada with her husband Frank, son Joshua and her dog Libby.

CALMING THE STORM

LISA ANDERSON

Self-control is strength;
Right Thought is mastery;
Calmness is power.

JAMES ALLEN

When I first lost control of myself, I was fourteen years old. I was saying goodbye to my friends at my front door when suddenly my hands and feet went numb and began to tingle. My chest felt heavy as if someone was sitting on it and squeezing the wind out of me. I began to hyperventilate. My heart sped up and it felt like it was pounding out of my chest. Terrified, I started shaking all over and I thought I was going to faint, or worse, die. Later I learned this was a panic attack. Back in the early 1980's, mental health was not taken as seriously as it is today and typically panic and anxiety were brushed off.

My parents came to see what was wrong with me. They thought I was exaggerating. People that have never experienced panic attacks don't realize how terrifying they can be. The more afraid and reactive you are in the moment of experiencing an episode, the more the symptoms intensify. My parents didn't know what to do and I certainly didn't either. I felt completely out of control and frightened. Then, as the evening went on, the symptoms subsided.

For two years I hardly gave a thought about panic attacks so when I started having them again, it completely caught me off guard. This time, they weren't random and they happened more and more often. At this point, I was in eleventh grade. I noticed that they happened when I was upset. My parents didn't like my boyfriend which caused us to have a lot of arguments. At my wits end between the panic attacks and the conflict with my parents, I packed my bag and ran away. Well, I didn't go too far. I stayed at a girlfriend's house with her family for three months. My parents saw that I had to leave to avoid more panic episodes. My attacks stopped so I broke up with my boyfriend and moved back home.

Time passed and I graduated high school. Like every summer since I was a child, my family went up north to our cottage. This was a special summer because being eighteen, it was the last full one that I could enjoy up there before going to college in September. I always loved the outdoors and the fun activities there. Life was awesome. My attacks were gone, I had control and my life back. I had a lot of friends at the cottage and that is when I started to date one of them. My parents were thrilled as they had known him and his family for a long time.

We dated for a few years and then became engaged. I couldn't have been happier. Once he put a ring on my finger, he started to tell me where we would be living and that I would have to leave my family. This made me nervous and I wasn't sure what to think. My family was so important to me and I didn't want to be away from them. Another odd thing was that he wasn't physical with me. He would pull away and I wondered what I was doing wrong. I expressed to him some of my concerns and he just shrugged his shoulders and didn't want to discuss it at all.

During a coffee break at work, I called my fiancé to say hi and see when he was coming over. Out of the blue, completely from left field, he told me it was over with no explanation. He broke it off, just... like... that. I wanted to say: *What the fuck? Are you fucking serious? On the phone? While I am at work?* I couldn't talk to him privately because I had coworkers beside me. I was stunned. A guy I had known almost my entire life does *this*? A man who I was supposed to marry? My brain was going a mile a minute. I began to hyperventilate and as I tried to catch my breath terrible sensations pummeled me. I didn't know what to do, I was scared, I was at work and it had been a long time since I had a panic attack. Panic attacks are unpredictable. They hit like a tsunami and leave as quickly as they arrive.

I was so afraid that my heart was going to burst and that I had a serious heart condition. I decided to go to the doctor about these episodes. After a series of tests and x-rays, the doctor concluded that I was healthy and "fine." I didn't feel fine but tried to learn to accept it.

The ex-fiancé fiasco was long behind me. I was working full-time, enjoying the single life, going out with friends on the weekends. The attacks were gone again and I was really enjoying life. Realizing that it was time for me to become more independent, I bought my uncle's car which gave me the freedom I loved and moved into a townhouse. I discovered that I really found living alone boring, so I found a girl to roommate with me. Everything was perfect.

Hanging out with the girls and clubbing Saturday nights were the thing to do. On this particular night, I ran into Adam, an old friend back from my school days. We danced all night and totally hit it off. We began to see each other regularly after that and he would often stay over at my place which caused conflict with my roommate. Eventually I asked her to leave and I moved back home to my parents' home. I didn't want to be alone and I didn't want my boyfriend moving in.

As time went by, Adam and I started to talk about marriage. He even moved across the street from my parents in a nice triplex apartment. Our relationship was great, we had a lot in common and we enjoyed the same activities. We were always going somewhere and doing something, we had so much fun together. We got engaged and I was afraid things wouldn't work out since I had been down this road before. I started sharing stories with my girlfriends that things seemed different, somewhat "off" with Adam and I wasn't sure what was going on. My intuition was warning me about something but I didn't know what. Adam was losing interest in doing anything. He was so moody and always seemed depressed and angry. I couldn't help but think, is it me?

My uneasiness about his behavior triggered me and the attacks started again. I still couldn't shake the feeling that something wasn't right with Adam. My "little birdie" as I called it, kept gnawing at me. All my life I referred to my intuition as my little birdie. In hindsight, I realize that every time I listened to my little birdie it was good and when I ignored it, things, let's just say, didn't work out. Your intuition is your gut telling you the truth. Trust your intuition because it will never let you down.

Well, this was one of those times that I didn't listen and ignored my gut. I just figured all was fine and it was just in my head. I mean, Adam never said anything was wrong and we saw each other every night. I decided that I would ease my mind and that we should talk about it over dinner. On this particular night we had plans to go out and I was looking forward to it. It would be the perfect opportunity to get some reassurance about things.

I popped over to his place after work and let myself in as I usually did. He was napping, so I woke him. He jumped up and started to scream at me. He pushed me to the floor. I got up and he shoved me over and over yelling at me and calling me names. I was trying to get to the door to get out and he pinned me against the wall. Adam held me there while he screamed in my face so I thrust my knee to his groin, although not hard, just enough to get away, at least that's what I wanted to happen. He had a grip of my arms, he banged me against the wall, threw me to the floor and start kicking me in the ribs over and over again. He was six-foot-two inches tall and towering over five-foot-three me. I fought with everything inside of me and managed to get out of his apartment, run across the street, and get to the safety of home.

I called my sister to come over and Adam's family to tell them what happened. My sister and his sister both came to my place while his dad went to his. I showed them marks on my body from him hitting and kicking me. Adam's dad found him hiding in the closet like a scared child, not like a man that should take responsibility for what he did. I told his family that the relationship was over and that I never wanted to see him again.

A few days after this happened Adam called me and asked me to give him a second chance. He told me he was sorry and would get help. I told him that I was glad he was getting help but there was no way I could go back after what happened.

I had to get out of the house so I called my girlfriends and a few of us went out. I also called Adam's mom as I could feel something was wrong. I didn't want to see his mom go over to Adam's since he was just across the street. I hoped by the time I got home she would not be around. However, when I got home there was an ambulance and two police cars across the street at his place and then I saw someone being carried out in a stretcher with IV and tubes all around. I lost it, my worse attack I ever had. I kept thinking oh my God what have I done, what had happened to him, will he survive? I watched out the window to see what was going on and it took everything in me not to run over. Maybe his mother was right. This was all my fault, what had I done!

I didn't get any sleep, it felt like the longest night of my life. My head was pounding and I couldn't stop crying. I was a wreck and knew that I couldn't work, so I called in sick. Three days later I finally found out what happened to him because he called me. Adam was in the hospital in a psychiatric ward. He had taken a bottle of Tylenol and drank a 24 case of beer. They found him half dead on his bathroom floor covered in vomit. He told me he damaged his liver and that if he ever touched another drop of alcohol, he would need a liver transplant. He also told me that he was an alcoholic. What?! How did I not know?

How can someone be an alcoholic without you knowing? Easily, they can hide it from anyone. When I would leave each evening to go home, he would sit and drink a case of beer. That explained a lot about the change in his personality, and things became clearer. He was so angry and moody and just couldn't wait for me to leave so he could drink. Imagine finding that out after we got married! Well, better before than after. Adam reassured me that he was getting all the help he needed. I was honestly happy for him.

This situation really took a toll on me. I needed help. My life was just going to work and sleeping. I wanted to be left alone. I lost total interest in everything and everyone. I was depressed and having panic attacks when I had to go to work. My mom started driving me because it was not safe for me to do it.

I went to the doctor and told him everything that happened. We had a great long talk. I told him that I blamed myself for everything that happened and my increased attacks that I couldn't control. This time the doctor didn't dismiss me and say it was nothing. He told me that I was having what is called a panic attack. This was the first time I had heard that term and an explanation for what I experienced.

Things for me began to get worse. I developed a generalized fear of everything. I was afraid to leave the house, get into my car, or even go to work. Every time I left the house, I would have a panic attack. I didn't want to go anywhere. My mom drove me to and from work. I did nothing else. I felt that I had no life and was just existing. Adam finally moved from across the street. I found that to be a huge relief. After a while of him being gone, the attacks stopped. It was time to fight for happiness again. I wanted my life back, I wanted me back. A girlfriend and I joined a gym together. I felt it was not only a great start to getting myself back on track health wise, but also a new place to meet people. I also really wanted to start dating again but not anyone I already knew. Time to start fresh.

The gym proved to be the positive step I needed to get my life back on track. I felt much more confident and in control of myself as I lost weight and started to look good too! The gym became my social life. I met a lot of new people both men and women. Every night I would go to the gym, work out and chat with everyone. I even felt healed from my past fiancé traumas. The friend I originally joined with stopped going but I met so many people that I was comfortable to go by myself. Life was back to being fun and exciting. I was even asked out for a date by a guy I met at the gym!

His name was Frank and our first date was the weekend of my parents' wedding anniversary as well the weekend my niece was born. I hoped that was a good omen! Our date was simple, yet magical as we went for a walk downtown. It started out as a hot summer evening and we hit it off. Out of the blue it started to pour and we ran for cover under a tree while we laughed our heads off. It was romantic. Standing under that tree I heard my "little birdie" inner-voice tell me that he's *"The One."*

Frank and I had a lot of fun together. We rode our bikes to the gym, worked out, and rode home. We went everywhere together. He enjoyed coming to the cottage and was right at home with my family. The more time we spent together, it became evident that we were meant for each other. I realized that all the bad things I went through brought me to this point in my life. It not only made me stronger, but I knew what I wanted in my future. Frank definitely was the one I wanted to marry.

That December Frank proposed to me, I was both excited and terrified. I knew what I wanted but what if something bad happens? All of the questions started up in my head again. I knew Frank wasn't like the others, but I couldn't help being afraid. Boom! That's when they started again. The uncontrollable attacks. Why does this keep happening to me? The anxiety and panic came back in a flurry. I didn't want to go anywhere or do anything. Most of all I was afraid Frank was going to call off our engagement.

I decided to go to the doctor because I didn't want this to ruin my relationship with Frank. He put me on Prozac for depression but I wasn't depressed. I was excited about getting married. It made no sense. Prozac stopped me from having the panic attacks but I found that I felt numb inside. I didn't feel any emotions at all, not happy, not sad... nothing. I knew I had to get off this medication because I didn't like how it made me feel. But what was the alternative?

My doctor sent me to so many specialists and nothing had worked until one day I was sent to a doctor who used hypnosis for his patients. I figured that I had tried everything, so I was open to being hypnotized. This doctor wanted to use hypnosis to take me back to the root cause of my panic attacks. This type of hypnosis is called Time Line Regression Therapy. True hypnosis is not the Hollywood Act that people often associate it to being. This is not entertainment and hypnosis will not make anyone do or say anything out of character. It taps into your free will. So, for example no one is going to quack like a duck in a bar. Hypnosis is not mind control, it actually is a state of calm and deep meditation. From there the licensed hypnotherapist will guide the client to tap into their buried unconscious mind to help with understanding and healing. That is where the work begins.

A hypnotherapist uses different techniques to help identify what the blocks are and why.

At the time, before I knew what hypnosis even was about and became a hypnotherapist, I was very surprised at what came out in my Time Line Regression Therapy session, because I truly believed that I healed from that childhood trauma. I thought about it from time to time but pushed down any emotions that I had to it. I tried hiding what happened my entire life.

When I was thirteen years old, Mike, my sister's boyfriend at the time, asked me to go for a ride in his cool car. I loved cars, so I just had to go! My sister set it up, so I knew it was ok. He picked me up down the street so my parents and neighbors couldn't see. Mike drove to his apartment and said he had to pick something up. He told me to come with him then motioned for me to sit on the sofa. He sat beside me and asked me my age and a lot of weird questions about dating. I thought to myself, I'm in eighth grade, how many dates does he think I go on? Mike told me he was twenty-five. He got up from the sofa, left the room, and called me over to follow him. My heart was pounding out of my chest.

I was terrified, so I did what he said. Mike grabbed my hand and forced me to touch him until he orgasmed. I just stood there staring out the window. I was horrified and felt myself shut down. I was crying and shaking, my heart pounding. I was in a panic and begged him to take me home. I didn't know if he would actually take me home or kill me. He did drive me home and I ran into the house. I told my sisters what happened. They told me to forget about it and never tell mom and dad or all of us would get into trouble. We never told.

It was our secret. It was my secret that I kept bottled up until I was twenty-five years old.

Once I got to the root of my attacks they stopped. I went off Prozac and felt relieved. It set me free. It was brought to my attention that I had a mild situational depression then. Therefore, Prozac helped me curb the anxiety and stopped the episodes to help me understand why I was having the panic attacks. Hypnotherapy tapped into my mind and uncovered what I thought I had already overcome years ago. My entire life I had tried to shut this horrible experience down, and hypnosis brought it to the forefront. Hypnosis made me realize that it was finally time for me to consciously deal with this trauma.

I have come to realize since doing the work on myself, that my reaction to each relationship was at the time, "what am I am doing wrong," and constantly blaming myself for the lack of respect I was receiving. Understanding that because of the sexual abuse event, I was afraid of being by myself and I never wanted to do anything alone. I was afraid to go out of my comfort zone and always needed a friend to be with me. I was also afraid that every man that I met, was just using me, that I didn't believe in my own value. Because I didn't have a self-worth, I had an internal longing for being wanted, desired, and taken care of… which meant marriage for security purposes.

Frank and I did get married for the right reasons, for true love. He was always different and treated me with respect. We each supported one another, communicated with each other and continued to enjoy each other's company. We had the same values which has built a strong marriage. We wanted to be parents, and together we endured fertility issues until we had our beautiful son, Joshua, who is now in his 20's. I loved every moment with my baby, so I quit my job to be a stay-at-home mom. Later, I decided to work part-time to get myself out of the house and find my own interests. I spent as much time as I could with my parents as well, as they were both elderly and sickly. My dad had been diagnosed with Alzheimer's and my mom with lung disease that required 24-hour oxygen. Not long after each being diagnosed, my parents died only six months apart from one another.

It was a double blow, basically losing both of my parents at what felt like the same time. Christmas was spent emptying out my parents' house. I was so depressed I gained a lot of weight, and lost interest in everything. I didn't care if I even got out of bed. I went on a leave of absence from the part-time job I once enjoyed so much. I knew I was clinically depressed and wondered if the panic attacks would come back, but thankfully they didn't. Looking at my situation, I realized I had only one choice: I had to get myself back up.

My little birdie told me that I needed hypnotherapy again. I believed in this healing method so much that I decided to go back to school and become a certified hypnotherapist. I used self-hypnosis to get my life back on track, lost eighty-five pounds, and I have never felt better in my life. I no longer have panic attacks and can even stand on stage in front of large groups for speaking engagements. My soul purpose and passion is to do the same for others and help them with their healing journey. I continued my studies and achieved a master hypnotherapist certification, 5-P.A.T.H. regression certification, sports hypnotherapy, and pain management hypnotherapy.

Hypnotherapy, saved my life. It also opened me up to become a healer myself and to help others to head in the right direction to fulfill their lives with the best quality of life. The healing process has given me an understanding that much of my stress and panic is because I felt out of control in situations at times in my life. The more I have had the confidence in myself, my life, and control of my reactions to situations and events, it has given me strength. I have been able to help myself and my clients to curb their emotional triggers.

We know that we cannot control what happens around us, but the power is in controlling ourselves to reacting or not. This helps with our anxiety. Self-control is so important and powerful in our thought processes. It is through hypnosis, meditation and positive thoughts that help in the creation for inner calmness. That inner calmness in itself is the power that will help in every aspect of our lives. It is the quiet confidence and inner strength that we make choices and decisions from that attribute to being happier in life and more fulfilled in our spiritual journey.

You can't calm the storm, so stop trying.
What you can do is calm yourself.
The storm will pass.
TIMBER HAWKEYE

RELAXATION AND LIFESTYLE TIPS

Here are some self-hypnosis and lifestyle tips that can help and that I use personally. Although these do not replace seeing a licensed hypnotherapist, mental health and/or heath care provider.

1

If you are experiencing a panic attack in a public place, try and find the quietest location you can, close your eyes, take a long deep breath and while you are inhaling count to 10. Exhale a long breath again counting to 10. Inhale count to 10 and exhale count to 10. Repeat three times or more depending on what you need.

2

If you are triggered at home, go to a room where you can be by yourself. Do the inhale and exhale exercise as above. While doing the breathing exercises, relax your body parts starting from your head to the tip of your toes. This can done sitting or lying down. Focus on each body part and then release the tension by continuing to deeply inhale and exhale.

3

Set a positive trigger for yourself: I have a stone bracelet, or you can even use a meditation ring. When you are feeling uncomfortable, experiencing any stress and/or anxiety, distract yourself by touching the bracelet, even moving the stones, like one would move a rosary. If you are using a meditation ring, touch the ring and spin it slowly around your finger. This distraction helps with reducing hyperventilation and brings about a calm and steady breathing pattern.

4

Ensure that you are eating a balanced diet. Avoid excessive sugar and caffeine as they both have been associated with panic attacks. Each in their own right can be part of your lifestyle (as long as your health care provider has approved it), however too much is not healthy and can make you jittery especially when consumed in the evening. This could also have effects on your sleep.

5

Incorporate daily body movement. This can be going up and down the stairs at home, finding an online exercise class based on your fitness level, going for a walk or run outside, or through finding an exercise class at the gym using cardio equipment, weight training; basically, anything that will help you move your body to its best ability. This will help you with stress and anxiety levels, confidence, motivation to help you feel better and has been known to increase positive mental health releasing of endorphins.

NATASHA AZADI

Natasha Azadi is a grieving mother, a private maternity nurse, and soul coach born in England. After the passing of her daughter in 2016, Natasha is a passionate, spiritual and multi-disciplinary certified soul coach helping others globally with their grief and loss. She currently lives in England and travels for work around the world.

FINDING HOPE

NATASHA AZADI

I had always spoken to spirits so it is no surprise that I always felt different to my family. In truth, I am. Very. The visitations from spirits started when I was a young child. My family told me that I was weird and odd when I started to express my experiences with the "other side." Overtime, I just stopped mentioning it. Seeing and hearing spirits never frightened me; I always found this gift a comfort.

I was a quiet child, choosing not to play outside with my sister, cousins and friends as I preferred to be by myself reading or chatting with my friends from beyond the grave. Although rare, I would have the odd encounter through sight, but mostly the connections would be auditory or a message would appear in my dreams. I remember being around eight years old and my great grandma Jessie coming to me in a dream to say she had passed and was back with grandad

Tommy and everything was ok. I knew as soon as I awoke, it wasn't an ordinary dream. I now know them to be visitation dreams. A short while later my older sister came to my room to tell me grandma had died and I remember casually saying "I know, she is ok though."

It is during this time in my childhood when I started to struggle with my emotions. Prior to this, I had been a very emotional and nervous child. Someone would look at me and I would cry, or just look away. I was made fun of for being too emotional by people, so I learned to hide how I felt and I became a master at it throughout my life.

Throughout my teenage years my relationship with my parents became rather strange. It would be fair to say that we didn't understand each other which caused fights and hardship. My parents both carried their emotional baggage from their childhoods into their adulthoods and it shaped them. As I grew, I noticed this and definitely didn't want to be like them. Also as I grew older, I found that as I learned to keep my emotions in check, I also lost my ability to communicate with the dead. I figured that somehow I had just switched off this communication channel.

As soon as I could, I dove head-first into education. I realized it was my way out. I could use it to change my life path. Spiritually speaking, it was the start of me breaking generations of unhealed trauma. By seeking my own truth and path in life I was shaking things up, and this was not a route I was expected to follow being from a small town in the north east of England. I studied hard, kept my head down, achieved what I was able, always pushing myself beyond what was expected of me. School and learning were my saviors. I always knew I wanted to work with children, so that is where my career initially led me to after school and college. I trained and worked in schools and nurseries, my favorite age being the first three years after birth.

LIFE BLESSINGS

As a young impressionable eighteen-year-old, I thought I knew all about life and the world. I was head strong, determined, a hard worker, and still loved education. In 2008, I met Christopher and began a whirlwind romance that resulted in us moving in together within six weeks, engagement that year, and marriage a year after that. We were completely in love and worshiped each other. We always spoke about having children and had never taken any precautions to prevent it from happening. Yet it wasn't until July 2011 that I became pregnant with my daughter, Jessica. It was a huge blessing but an equally big shock as we had never gotten pregnant in all of our years together prior to that. Months upon months of pregnancy tests all negative, then—bam, a positive. I was super thrilled and really nervous.

We were really excited about becoming parents. All I have ever wanted was to become a mother so this was a dream come true. I didn't have the easiest of pregnancies due to complications with sickness, bleeding, and being told I had Group B Strep. Group B Strep was potentially life-threating to my daughter and to protect her I was given antibiotics during labor and I knew that shortly after birth, she would also need them.

I went into labor prematurely in the thirty-sixth week of pregnancy. Birth was the easiest part as it lasted only an hour, but during the whole agonizing time, I was also grieving my niece who had been stillborn five days prior to going into my own premature labor.

I was absolutely terrified I too was going to lose my daughter. But at 10:52 a.m. February 24th, 2012, the midwife handed me my beautiful baby girl, all six pounds of her, a mass of jet-black hair with the chubbiest cheeks. There she was—just staring at me. Upon my first look at her, I fell in love and all my worries melted away. It was in that moment I truly knew what deep unconditional love was and a bond between us was formed, a bond unlike any I had ever experienced in my life. She was mine and I was hers.

Jessica was a very happy go lucky girl, an absolute angel. As she grew, she would light up each room she entered with her smile. She had an amazing sense of humor and an infectious laugh. Anyone who met her fell in love instantly. Jessica was so friendly that she would talk to anybody.

BROKEN BUT NOT ALONE

Christopher and I experienced marital issues that became more prominent in 2015; our marriage was crumbling. My life was Jessica and home. She was my world and all that I cared about. I threw everything I had into motherhood. My roles as mother, wife, and homemaker all took priority over running my own business. Looking back, I see we both neglected the marriage. I did by putting Jessica first. Christopher also did by working offsite out of town so often and when he was home, he continued to be more interested in business meetings than his family. We had gotten to the point where we fought constantly, agreed on nothing, and everything was a huge battle between us. We both knew it was over but kept it going longer for Jessica. I never wanted her to come from a "broken home" like mine. I wanted her to have both parents, stability, and most importantly a loving home.

The pressure and strain of me not being able to conceive another child was also a major factor in the breakdown of our marriage. I blamed him, he blamed me. We had tests and it turned out that I was the issue, but at that moment in time I was happy with what we had. I always felt blessed to have Jess and Christopher also had a daughter from a previous relationship. I didn't want rounds of IVF. I was happy with our girls.

Christopher moved out of our family home in August 2016. During this time nobody other than our parents knew that we had separated, because we were due to go on a big family holiday with his side of the family, so I was asked to keep it quiet, which I did. The secrecy and the separation caused me considerable emotional stress and trauma, which led me to actually being ill most of the holiday. I didn't get married for it to end in divorce, no matter how bad the situation.

I started seeing a therapist immediately after the breakdown of our marriage. I thought I needed to fix myself and if I also fixed the emotional issues which I was constantly told I had, then maybe my marriage could be saved. But it couldn't. In the end we couldn't make it work. Ten years of marriage gone, finished. I was broken but I wasn't alone. I still had my girl, who was my world and my life.

TRAGEDY STRIKES

Only a month after the separation, on September 9, 2016, tragedy struck and in a split second, my entire world collapsed. My beautiful four-year-old Jessica died in my arms at home after a fall in the garden caused her irreversible head injuries. I watched the life drain from her body and her eyes. As any mother would, I tried my best to save her, even though I knew she had gone. I had seen her soul leave her body, but I just couldn't believe it. I didn't want to believe it. She was all I had left in the world and just like that she was gone. I restarted her heart with CPR, but I knew, being pediatric first-aid trained, that the type of blood coming from her ears, nose, and mouth was from a severe brain bleed. Shortly after our arrival at the hospital, Jessica was pronounced dead. I often describe it as the moment I died too, but somehow my heart kept on beating.

I still have dreams/nightmares of those words echoing at me, "I'm so sorry, but she has gone." It is any parents' worst nightmare, one that has no ending. Words cannot describe the pain of losing a child. It is not the natural order of things and there really aren't any words of comfort to a grieving parent.

I remember just being numb with shock. I needed to see her, to touch her, to hold her. Eventually I got to. I climbed into the bed with her for what seemed like hours. I washed her down and I brushed her hair. She really looked like she was asleep. My perfect sleeping angel.

Later that evening, Christopher and I were told they needed to take her to the bereavement suite. I was handed a memorial box, with hand and footprints, a lock of her hair, a poem, candle, two teddies, and a memory stick. I was also given a leaflet on how to cope with a loss and we left. We stood outside the hospital wondering, "What do we do now?" Nothing explained, no real support was offered. We got to see her for one hour each day over the weekend before she was taken for an autopsy. As she was a child under eighteen who died suddenly, that is natural procedure in the UK.

The undertaker brought her home to us for four days before her funeral. I spent every second by my baby's side, making sure she was just perfect. Holding her hand every moment I could. Soaking in every feature of hers, as I knew the funeral was fast approaching and I would never get to gaze upon her beautiful face again nor would I be able to touch her or hold her hands again.

The day of the funeral came far too soon. That morning I applied her favorite lip gloss on her lips, dressed her in her princess gown, wrapped her in her favorite princess blanket surrounded by teddies, letters, snacks. I also gave her a lilac eternal rose. The undertaker collected her and took her away in the hearse to the church service and then to the burial site.

The funeral came and went. My entire world was Jessica and now she was just gone; I was in our home alone. I was lost completely in my own mind, which for me is a dangerous place to be. I just wanted to die, but I didn't want my parents to feel the pain that I felt by losing Jessica. So, I continued therapy, drank a lot, and secluded myself away from everyone. Most of my time was spent at Jessica's grave, but I hate calling it that so I have always called it her "forever bed." For me, that's where her body sleeps, the body I gave birth to, the body that made me a mother, and where I will go when my time comes.

I went to stay with my parents. I took the numerous pills prescribed by my doctor, but nothing helped. Nothing could stop me longing for my child to be back in my arms, for my life to return to normal. I didn't want to be here in the world anymore. I was in such a deep dark place and I had no idea how to escape it and I never thought I would. The thing is with grief from the loss of a child, that hole always stays with you. You just have to learn to navigate around it and not fall in and drown, which I have nearly done on numerous occasions.

WHO AM I?

Around three months after Jessica's passing, I decided to make some changes in my life. I threw myself back into education to retrain in something that would take me away from my life at home. I wanted to have a new purpose and focus. I already had a whole range of courses/ training behind me and a close friend mentioned maternity nursing. This sounded great as I love children. I became a maternity nurse so I could help and teach new mothers how to be the best parents they can be. I showed them how they could have a beautiful, contented baby.

My job has taken me all over the world in the last four years and I do love it. It is extremely hard work being on shift up to twenty hours a day six days a week. I worked pretty much ten months of the year, with a week here and there at home because being at work is the greatest escape from my life and reality. At work I am just Natasha the maternity nurse, at home I am Natasha the grieving mother. I don't have to divulge my life to my clients if I don't wish to and some don't ask personal questions. Those that have asked, I always talk about Jessica and my life, plus what happened as she is still my child and I am still her mother.

Life at home was difficult because over time people expect you to be "ok." People expect you to have gotten over the death of your child, and to have moved on. The more people expect you to be ok, the more you pretend you are ok. I found myself for years just saying, "I'm ok" or "I'm fine" as people really don't want to hear that you are not doing well so I could not share that I was absolutely breaking down inside. What I showed to the world outwardly was not what I was feeling inside.

I didn't feel like a mother anymore, but yet I still bought things for Jessica for her forever bed. Her room and garden at home are the same as the day she left. I was massively struggling. I couldn't bear the emptiness and loneliness I felt at home and inside my own body and I felt nobody understood and nobody cared. In 2018, I had a complete breakdown and tried to end my own life, landing me a short stay in hospital. It was a mixture of complete exhaustion from work and unbearable grief—I didn't know who I was anymore. If I wasn't a mother, what was I? Who am I?

I thought there was a timeline to grief and that you had to grieve a certain way. I was walking around, trying to find my place in the world, to fit in with everyone else's expectations of me. Pleasing only them and not myself, giving everything I had and leaving myself empty. I didn't know how to grieve for Jessica or even for the person I was before I lost her. This has only been a realization I have had in the last twelve months, three years after her death.

FINDING MYSELF AND MY SOUL

If someone would have told me that 2020 was going to be the year of my spiritual awakening, I would have laughed and called them crazy. But this is where I have found myself. A journey to the soul, connection, embracing the spirit world, self-love and acceptance. This has been a year of deep healing, acknowledging I too am important, that I have a life worth living, and learning to take back my own power. It was the year of journey, into really grieving for my child. I have opened myself up to the spirit world, partaking in new learning, and I started collecting numerous crystals, books, and tarot cards.

It all started in October 2019 with a random message that Jessica had come through to a medium at a spiritual demonstration, one which I was actually meant to attend, but for some reason didn't go. Then a phone call in December of that year led me to a demonstration of mediumship and in January 2020 I went for a private reading. That meeting was fabulous, the medium and I chatted for a while and she mentioned "soul work for healing."

I didn't know what it was as I had never really heard of it but a seed had been planted. I knew this because over the coming weeks and months I would randomly think about it. I was interested and intrigued, and me being me, did a little research. I tossed the idea back and forth, sometimes I was like "yes this is for me." Other times, I thought there was no way I could do it—that it was too scary to open myself up like that and that there was no way I could allow myself to be that vulnerable. It was the unknown and I had no idea what to expect, but I decided to at least try it. By the end of April 2020, I was ready to consider a change. I contacted the lady about doing some soul work as I was due back from working away and thought it might be an ideal time to start something new.

Wednesday the 10th of June 2020 is the day my world changed forever for the better. I started guided meditation soul work. In my first session I experienced something which I have never lost and only built upon since then: a connection to Jessica's spirit and other passed family members. I have also had messages for other people and have passed those on, where I felt it necessary. I didn't expect to find that I had psychic abilities again. I started and continue soul work for me to heal from past trauma. My soul work has brought me to the spirit world and Jessica and it has also reconnected me back to what I could sense, see, and feel as a small child. I believe I have found my soul purpose. I am living my truth in helping others who are grieving, and I use my abilities to connect with the spirit world to do this. I have always been empathic and very sensitive, and now understand why. Because I understand loss at a deeper level, I am able to have a more compassionate and trusting approach. My soul coaching practice provides readings for people who wish to connect with their loved ones.

I knew Jessica also had the gift from an early age which I only encouraged and nurtured, in a way that I was not. She would talk about her past lives, with names, dates, and places and even how she had passed away. She also spoke about my great grandparents visiting her often, plus a little boy, George, who she told me also lives in our home. The spirit world has never scared me, it only brought my imagination and creativity to life. Reconnecting to my daughter's spirit, has brought me so much joy. For in life and even in her death, we are and will always be "two hearts one soul, connecting for eternity."

I am constantly learning and growing. Jessica is always at home or traveling with me. I feel her more when I'm in a good place. I can also hear and talk with her without having to connect through meditation, as I have to with other spirits. Missing Jessica in the physical is something I still struggle with—naturally, as she is my child. That is also part of openly grieving and healing, but I know I am so incredibly blessed to be able to connect to the spirit world. I am now working on finding a balance, but it's all learning, healing and growing. My favorite motto is "you have to feel it to heal it."

Learning to being open and trusting to let somebody get close to me has been a massive step for me. In this, I have also found a true friend who accepts me for all my flaws, never judges, and only nurtures and encourages me to keep going and move forward. This has given me a freedom in another way. This connection shows me that I'm actually not a bad person, I am worthy, I am lovable, and I shouldn't hide away from the world because of the past. There is another who now loves me. The saying that you can pick your friends but not your family is true; however, that also depends on your definition of family. Do they have to be blood? *No.* I get to choose who I want in my life for good and that, to me, is creating for myself a new family, consisting of only pure souls. As a family we can learn from each other, support, guide, help, cry, and heal. Most importantly, we can love each other wholeheartedly without fear of rejection or judgment.

Looking back at the changes within myself, I can see that it has been quite rapid and extraordinary. My life has certainly come with its share of challenges, emotional highs and lows, grief and loss. I never could have imagined where soul work would or could lead me. My journey is far from over, and it is one of the craziest emotional rollercoaster rides I have ever had the privilege to be on.

To know I am not alone on this side and the other side has made my life a little more bearable. There are times I do still feel alone, when everything from within life falls on top of me and I can't see a way out. But healing isn't linear, and I am grieving my only child. There is no right or wrong way to grieve. We will all do it in a way which is right for us. My grief and your grief are as individual as our fingerprints. It is healthy to grieve openly, even if the world doesn't understand. I created my Instagram page early in 2020 as a dedication to my grieving and soul journey. I have made connections to so many grieving parents, brothers, sisters, and grandparents who all share one common factor: They are grieving. No matter how you grieve or what trauma you have been through, your pain is valid, and nobody has the right to tell you it isn't. It is important to have a safe platform for people to grieve openly without judgment with only compassion and understanding.

My mission is to get people talking about grief and loss in all areas of life. We are all human and we will all experience grief in our lifetime. It shouldn't be a taboo subject—especially child loss. I am hopeful for a new future where I will turn my pain into power and use my voice. Staying connected to my soul and to the spirit world is what I need to do. It is showing me a strength I never knew I had. It's not an easy process. It's messy, complicated, and downright tough.

I'm learning to take each day as it comes and to surround myself in kindness while I'm healing. I'm starting to see the light and I am letting it in. I'm moving forward slowly but surely, holding my head high with my arms open wide to accept the future, friendship, family, and the life I never believed I could or deserved to have. For me, it's not just about the spirit world. Spirituality and daily meditation has to become part of my every day practice to give me a clearer view of life. This helps me to remain calm and eases my anxiety and the panic attacks I've suffered since Jessica's accident. It also gives me a deeper emotional intelligence, helps me remain centered to myself and to be grounded. It gives me increased intuition and helps create a more positive mindset, increasing my self-confidence. Through meditation, I connect to my soul and I do a lot of inner child healing work, to help change my negative thinking patterns which have an effect on my day-to-day life. Finding peace and balance in life is what everyone should know about and have access to, if they wish.

Again, I have turned to education. I'm currently undertaking a whole range of courses from spiritual life coaching, meditation practitioner, hypnotherapy, past life regression, soul retrieval, and mindfulness to name a few. Most recently, I have been announced a finalist for the Centre of Excellence's, "Inspiration of The Year" Award.

We all have the ability to connect, you just have to have an open mind and an open heart as my wonderful mentor says, and she is absolutely right. It's not all about connecting to the spirit world but connecting to your core self, your soul; it has so many physical and mental benefits. It's helped me so much on my journey. I want to give this gift to others to help heal them in some way, to bring some peace to others through their loss and heartache.

We never "get over" the loss of a child. It isn't only the biological parents that have lost a child. The loss is also affects grandparents, step-parents, siblings, blended families, aunts, and uncles, and friends who can be as close as family. For those grieving individuals and families all over the world, I want to provide hope, love, and understanding for a better tomorrow.

My message to all grieving hearts across the world is I want you to know I see you, I feel you, and I am here with you. You are not alone. We are never alone as our loved ones may be gone in the physical, but their souls/spirit continue on. There is no death. Love never dies. Their souls are with us, every step of the way. Our grief is the price we pay for love. We loved our children in life, and we love them still after their physical body is gone. Be proud and say their names, even if others don't want to hear, or if they feel uncomfortable by you mentioning your dead child. Remember this, they only feel uncomfortable for a moment, we have to live uncomfortably all the time knowing that our child no longer lives on Earth but is instead in heaven always watching and always guiding us. Say their name and share your memories proudly.

RANJINI CASSUP

Ranjini Cassup is a serial entrepreneur and life coach with over twenty years of experience with start-ups and business transformation. She has dedicated herself to empowering women through personal and business coaching as well as being an active volunteer and mentor. Her personal experiences have enabled her to see life through a lens of understanding with no judgment.

BREAKING EVERY RULE

RANJINI CASSUP

*Know the rules well, so you
can break them effectively.*

DALAI LAMA

I have heard it said that our souls choose our earth families and life
circumstances based on the lessons they need to learn. Perhaps my
soul was busy star gazing, missed the instructions, or had a very sick
sense of humor. For some reason, I couldn't wait to start living this
earthly existence. I arrived ten weeks early weighing just over three
pounds. Born to a newly married immigrant couple from Fiji, who
were still learning about themselves, their new country, and the perils
of life. Home from the hospital, I was delivered right to the loving
arms of my grandmother, who relished every moment spent with me
and taught me a love so pure, so unconditional that nine short years
with her would be enough to fill me up for a lifetime.

My last weekend with my Goody Amma (my name for her) was
not unusual or complicated. It was spent cooking and cleaning. The

only difference was the short and unassuming conversation we had about life... and death. I remember her handing me a little package full of trinkets. She looked at me so intently and said, "I don't want you to cry when I die. I want you to be a good girl, be strong, be happy and know that I will never be far, even if I am not here." It was the last time I saw her; she died the next morning. And just like that, everything changed.

I suppose up until that point I didn't really know my parents. I mean I spent the week with them, they clothed me, and fed me, and made sure I went to school, but they had two other kids that demanded their attention and they both worked full-time. I was the eldest and was expected to help; to be seen and not heard. My parents were very strict and had may unwritten rules that we needed to live by, including ones on how we should behave.

My father started drinking shortly after my grandmother died. It is also when I started to notice the fighting. I could hear my parents going at it *all the time*. The crying and screaming coming from the bedroom in the middle of a Sunday afternoon and the anger and shame on my mother's face as she beelined to the bathroom to wash it away. Nothing could be done to drown out the noise in our tiny apartment. It simply became normal. Perhaps my little soul had considered this amongst its first lesson for life on earth: ignore what is and just keep moving.

The drinking became constant and the heaviness in the air could be felt the moment he walked in the door. Sundays were terrible, but that particular Sunday was the worst. We had just finished lunch. My mother sent my brother and sister into the basement to watch TV as she angrily made her way upstairs to the bedroom. This had become part of the Sunday routine. I consistently applied unwritten rule number one: "ignore and carry on." I became an expert at blocking out the screams and physically blending into the background. "Don't be seen, don't be heard," became rule number two.

I don't know what got into me that day. As I was wiping off the table, I mindlessly threw a fork into the sink. As soon as I heard the loud clang of the fork hitting the stainless-steel sink, I knew I was in trouble. Rule number two had been broken, I had been heard and now I would be seen. My ten-year-old body shook in fear. I froze, afraid to move or make another sound.

I felt my hair being pulled so hard that I thought my head would detach from my neck, then my face hit the fridge. I nearly blacked out as I fell to the floor. I instinctively reached out with my hand, trying to use the table to break my fall. From the floor, I saw the metal legs of the kitchen chair coming towards me as he picked it up and hit me with it, over and over again. The table was on its side by this point and I was curled in a ball against it, his foot kicking me in my back, my head, stomping on me. I could hear my mother and siblings screaming for him to stop. He didn't. Drifting in and out of consciousness, I remember laying in pool of blood and urine. I remember the smell of my own feces and then I remember everything going black.

I woke up in my own bed, with my throbbing head on my blood-stained pillow. I had no idea how much time had passed. The pain was so unforgiving that I wished I was dead, but the physical was not the worst part. My mother hadn't called an ambulance or the police or anyone once she saw that I was alive. She cried and told me that it was my fault for making so much noise to begin with.

Over the next five years, the beatings got worse and became more consistent. It was just something we came to expect. There was no peace in our home unless he was not there. I started to understand that my mother, like me, had learned to live by these unwritten rules. Without even speaking, my mother passed down rule number three: "once you get married, that's it." You are forever obligated to put up with any and all shit your husband throws your way. Divorce is not an option and how things look is more important than how they really are.

I was fifteen when I found my courage. My scheduled shift at McDonalds finished and I headed home. In my head was a vision of a house, our house. It was perfection to look at, one with a huge foyer and a balcony that overlooked from upstairs. In this house, the sound traveled and echoed in the high ceilings, everything was white, everything matched and had a place. Symbolically it embodied "the North American dream." Rule four was probably the most important rule of all. "Work hard, buy all the stuff and don't let anyone know what happens in your home." How it looks is more important that how it is. The value of living was more important than the value of life.

I saw the blood as soon as I walked in. I heard the screams coming from the master bedroom and I saw the fear in my little sister's and brother's eyes. I ran upstairs to see him bashing her head against the toilet. I quietly left the room and dialed 911. The police came, they questioned my mother, and of course… she lied. They arrested him anyway. I stood on the front porch as they escorted him to the car. He looked directly at me and calmly said, "you fucking bitch, the next time I see you, I'm going to kill you."

I believed him.

I left that day with nothing more than a few outfits. A cousin came and collected me. She let me stay at her home until I turned sixteen a few months later. I found two jobs, a friend who was willing to share the rent, and got my own place. I was safe. I was happy. I was free.

NEW SNEAKERS AND A SMILE

Something so new, yet so familiar…
almost like I met him in another lifetime.

I met the love of my life when I was eighteen. He literally walked into my apartment and changed everything for me. A vison of perfection, fresh white sneakers, without a scuff to be seen. He had on the trendiest jean suit that was about three sizes too big, flawless dark skin, and a perfect smile. The only thing missing was the halo and heavenly music. There was just something about him. Every bit of common sense I had disappeared instantly—like, it simply vanished! It was love at first sight. This man was about to change the trajectory of my entire life. You see, until that point all males had been kept at an arms-length. Marriage was not for me. I was not my mother. I was not going to let something as fleeting as love get in the way of my dreams. Or so I thought.

THE FIRST TIME

It is so easy to give other people good advice,
why is it so hard to give it to yourself?

Our life was good. We were in love. By the time I was twenty-three, we had two beautiful daughters, had purchased our first home, we had a trucking business that he ran, and I had a full-time job in an office. Neither one of us went to college; we couldn't afford it. And in the spirit of like attracting like, we both had a predisposed notion of what success meant and were willing to do what it took to get there and stay there.

Then I got the call from his cousin. I needed to make my way down to City Hall to post bail as he had been arrested for possession of narcotics. I could not understand what was happening, but still posted bail and agreed to all the conditions. This had to be a mistake—but it wasn't. I found out that he had been involved in this "world" for a few months prior to his arrest.

I was beyond angry and hysterical. He cried, apologized, and swore up and down that it wouldn't ever happen again. Yet not even six months later, he was arrested a second time but denied bail this time. He was not released from jail and they were saying he was the center of a sting operation. What the actual fuck was happening? Who the fuck was this man and how in the hell was he a fucking "King Pin" when we stretched each month to pay our bills and budgeted for groceries?

It happened so fast. I received the call to come to the police station, not to post bail, but to turn myself in. They said that as I was his "wife," I was guilty by association. I dropped my children off with my sister who still lived at home with my parents.

They charged me in an effort to get him to plead guilty. I was naïve and had never been in trouble with the law before. I learned quickly that the police were using me as a pawn to force him to plead guilty. In lieu of an immediate bail hearing, there was a ten day wait in which they transferred me to a maximum-security women's prison in the middle of nowhere. This experience certainly opened my eyes to a life I wanted no part of. At my bail hearing, I was granted house arrest and released into the custody of... my father. That in itself was worse than jail as my father was relentless in his constant threats to pull my bail, taunting me and physical abusive. How the fuck did I get here?

A year passed. Although the police had lost most of the physical evidence (including the drugs and car) and two of the officers had been charged with corruption, it was not enough. We simply did not have the money to keep fighting and pay lawyers. He ended up taking a plea deal so that they would finally release me from my sixteen months of hell. He was sentenced to two years and sent to a minimum-security facility where he served nine months and was released.

I thought a lot about my stupidity. I mean, did I love this man so much that I was blind to see the signs leading up to the first arrest? The details were clear. No, he wasn't the King Pin; he picked up and dropped off packages in exchange for a few hundred dollars to make ends meet for our family. Could he have found another way? Of course. But in his mind, he simply did what he had to do to provide for us.

I realized that he was not the perfect man that I created in my mind. I saw what I chose to see. Yes, he was kind, gentle, a wonderful father, and great friend. He was always respectful, never harsh. He told me he loved me each and every day. But he also had a skewed definition of what it meant to be a man and he sheltered me from that truth. He had a wandering eye that everyone seemed to know about except me. You see, where he came from "real men" did whatever they had to do to provide for their wives and had sweethearts on the side.

STARTING OVER

Making mistakes are evitable, it is the lesson that matters. Some learn quickly... others not so much.

After his release from prison, he took a full-time job driving a truck and assembling office cubicles. That first year, we saved every single penny he earned. In October of 2005, we opened our first restaurant. It was his dream come true as he was a passionate cook. He went to school part-time to learn the trade and our restaurant quickly became the go-to place for great Jamaican food.

Things were going well. We finally got married in 2006. It all seemed to be coming together. He continued to be who he was, and I choose to only see the good. I ignored his immaturity and his wandering eye. In hindsight, I didn't feel that I deserved more. Honestly, I thought, who was I to think that I could have more? Plus, I had achieved success by every other standard. I was married with two kids, a dog, a beautiful home, a vacation home in the Caribbean, five cars, a successful restaurant, and a catering business. I had a dream job doing what I loved and earning more money than I thought possible for an uneducated girl like me. I volunteered my time and gave generously. I was not going to rock this boat. I choose to live this way. As long as it was perfect on the outside, what was happening inside of me didn't matter. Apply the rules girl! Don't make a sound and don't create a fuss. Accept what is and keep it moving! But life had other plans. Life had decided that it was finally time to unlearn the lessons taught to me so long ago.

TWO DIFFERENT PLANETS

Our roots were intertwined.
We had grown up together,
how had we grown so far apart?

More than 20 years had passed since that first smile. We had survived what seemed like the worst. The Universe had blessed us with a second chance and we thrived. We took nothing for granted. Life was good and the blessings continued to flow—we were in the law of attraction. Opportunities came out of nowhere, so when we heard that a song that he had casually recorded and released (did I mention that music was his hobby?), had gone to the top of the Dancehall charts—we thought, *This is it! This is that once in a lifetime opportunity to live your dream!*

And it all happened so fast—the calls to shows, touring and endorsements. We already had a home in Jamaica, our eldest was away at university, with the second one soon to follow. I had started my consulting company, finally breaking free from the chains of the 9:00 to 5:00. The timing couldn't be more perfect.

We sold our home, downsized our life, and he left to start his new adventure, pursuing his music career with his home base in Jamaica. Our agreement was one year. We had given ourselves one year for living apart. We agreed that I would stay back to tie up loose ends here and ensure our girls had what they needed. One year gave him the time to focus solely on building his brand without distraction. One year.

One year turned into four years. I convinced myself that I couldn't leave. I had all the excuses: my business was flourishing, my volunteer communities needed me, and the kids needed me. Truth is, I had worked so hard for this success. I could not just up and leave it all behind, not yet. This was the first and only thing in my life that I had built on my own. I was really proud of myself and accomplishments.

My husband pleaded with me to join him to start fresh and enjoy life together—just him and I. We had checked the boxes, did all the things, raised the kids, and provided a good strong foundation for them. We had the money and we were still young enough to enjoy it. We even opened our second restaurant, this one in Jamaica, and it was thriving. What was I waiting for?

I cried a lot that year. I was lonely but yet I continued to choose loneliness. Why didn't I believe that I deserved this life? This life that we had built and planned for, was laying at my feet and I chose to not pick it up. We saw each other for a few days once per month. Obviously, that didn't constitute a happy marriage for us.

My husband grew more distant. He was used to a busy home. He was used to cooking and cleaning, planning, and providing. He was finally able to give me the life of leisure that I said I wanted… yet I continued to choose everything but him. Perhaps subconsciously I wanted to prove that I could survive on my own. Maybe I wanted him to miss me and feel that pain that he had caused me so many times. Maybe I was scared to be happy.

I suggested a legal separation perhaps even divorce. It just seemed like the right thing to do, not because it was what either of us wanted it, but it continued in the cycle of chaos that felt normal to me. Rule five was one I had taught myself: "don't get too comfortable." Find away to ruin it before it ruins you. Happiness was not for people like me. I didn't deserve it. I was not worthy of it.

BONUS BABY

There is a silver lining in everything, if you look hard enough.

A year into this separation bullshit, we realized that we did in fact love each other and our life, with all of its imperfections, was worth trying for. While I was still not ready to make a full-time transition to the land of wood and water, I started to work remotely, spending months at a time with my husband. It felt fresh and new. I was happy. We were happy, and then the actual bomb dropped. Nothing in my life could have prepared me for the explosion that came. While we were separated, he met someone. She got pregnant and they had a son.

He explained that he could not find the moment or the words to tell me sooner. He said that everything between us was perfect, for the first time in such a long time. He didn't want to risk losing me or our family, but he also could not deny his son a father. Something he never had.

The aftermath was real. I had no tears, just anger. How could he have kept this from me? How did he manage all these months, when committed to building a new foundation, to lie to me? To lie to our kids? To lie to our family? I was hurt. I had been betrayed. Not because he had slept with someone else while we chose to be apart, but because he had not told me.

Time passed and eventually I agreed to speak to him again. Actually, he gave me no choice this time. He followed me on a pre-planned trip to Hong Kong, and we finally talked… about everything. No holds barred, no fear of judgment, no expectations. Just raw honest, emotional conversation.

We agreed that to have any resemblance of a relationship, even a friendship, we needed counseling. We needed to purge these old ideas that we had planted in our minds. We needed to dig up and do away with these seeds that no longer served us, burn the roots and plant new seeds. Sometimes the only way up is to start face down in the mud covered in shit. I had so much to unlearn. We had so much to unlearn. We embarked on the journey together, roots intertwined. Raw, exposed and emotionally naked.

We learned to talk and have real conversations, not words full of fluff and pretense. We learned to talk about our fears, our failures, and our successes. We realized that all along we had been living to a standard taught to us by others. Our own definition of success, the one we could agree on was happiness. Whatever that looked like.

Today, we have learned to live in the moment. We realize that there were many things that we should have done differently, but we also know that the lessons were needed to be where we are now.

Happy.

EPIPHANY

My Soul Lessons are part of my journey and I know there are more coming in the future. The real lessons were simple:

LESSON 1

Love unconditionally. Always.

LESSON 2

You are stardust, made perfectly in the image of the creator. You are meant to be seen and to be heard.

LESSON 3

You come first—always. You can't fill another if you're empty.

LESSON 4

True success does not come in the form of material things.

LESSON 5

Everything in life is a choice. You choose the trajectory of your life and you can't blame life (or anyone else for that matter) for the choices that you make or the things you choose to live with.

LESSON 6

Don't wait for someone to tell you that you are worthy. Wake up every day and tell yourself!

LESSON 7

Don't judge others. We simply don't know what leads people to make the choices they make. We don't know what they have learned along the way or the things they are sacrificing to have what they have.

LESSON 8

You can't change anyone: Change yourself.

LESSON 9

Life is forgiving. Learn to forgive yourself.

LESSON 10

Do what brings you joy even if it makes sense to no one else.

LESSON 11

Life is not complicated. We make it complicated by putting too much value on the opinions of others.

LESSON 12

Being happy has no prerequisite. You can choose happiness today, regardless of what happened yesterday.

LESSON 13

Love yourself freely and accept everything that you deserve.

LESSON 14

Forgive, give grace, and do not cast judgment on anyone or any situation.

LESSON 15

Give generously and keep trying even when it seems impossible.

LESSON 16

There is light in every lesson; you just have to look.

LESSON 17

Even if you feel terrible today or you're in the worst season of your life know that every storm runs out of rain and the sun always comes out.

LESSON 18

Live in the present. Enjoy today without worrying about tomorrow. Every day is a new day, a new opportunity full of new blessings.

LESSON 19

Life will continue to have many ups and downs, but know that you can choose your reaction to everything that happens around you. The burden of hatred is far too heavy to carry each day. What happened in the past, happened. You can't change that, but your past does not define my future.

LESSON 20

I have found a new love with an old friend and it is beautiful. Our blended family of grown adult children and a three-year-old is unconventional and seems impossibly crazy to some people, but we live life on our own terms. The lesson is to live freely without care or concern for what people think, their opinions of you and how you live are their business, not yours.

I have broken every rule to get here and in hindsight, I had gotten life so wrong. I had learned survival, and everything I have learned along the way, has made me the woman I am today.

The soul would have no rainbow,
had the eyes no tears.
JOHN VANCE CHENEY

JENNIFER CHAPMAN

Jennifer Chapman, is a published author and a licensed coach with Just Commit Coaching. She is passionate about working and supporting others globally who want to break through life's challenges. She currently lives in Indianapolis, Indiana, USA with her husband.

SURVIVE TO THRIVE

JENNIFER CHAPMAN

Growing up with wonderful parents, a younger brother, and close family was a dream. I played outside, rode bikes, went to the lake on weekends, and simply loved life. My passions as a kid were dancing, softball, and tennis. I was always active and going to a practice, tournament, or recital and was extremely tenacious; I was driven to win, whether in school or after school activities. My family was always supportive of me, especially my mom—my number one cheerleader. It meant so much to have the family love and guidance that I had. It was this foundation of family support aligned with my strong competitive nature that helped me thrive after a devastating loss and later survive a life changing event myself that has shifted my whole perspective.

My dream life as I knew it changed when I was eleven years old. The summer before sixth-grade we hosted a family cookout. We spent time outside and had a meal together like we had done hundreds of times. This one was different. After dinner, my mom disappeared to her bedroom. We hadn't seen her for a while, so we went to check on her. There she was, she had vomited and was passed out on the bathroom floor. We called the ambulance. My brother and I were terrified and hysterical. My aunt and grandparents surrounded us and assured us everything was going to be ok.

My mom was transported to a hospital and us to our grandparents' house. We did not know much about what was happening from one minute to the next. It was a full thirty-six hours later, before we found out how bad the situation was. I was woken up by my dad, early in the morning. He tearfully said, "Mom did not make it." *Wait... what?* I thought. I literally could not wrap my head around the fact that she was perfectly fine two nights before and was now gone. I was shattered.

The next couple of days were a whirlwind of activities. There I was, eleven years old, walking into a funeral home to say goodbye to my mom. It was gut-wrenching. It was also heartbreaking to see my brother, my father, and other family members doing the same thing. The amount of support shown to us was overwhelming. There was a line out the door where, for four straight hours, we met with family, friends, and acquaintances who brought cards, flowers, love, and condolences to our family.

One of the hardest moments during this time was having to see my dad break down as we said our final goodbye. From that point on, every time we would go "visit" her as a family, he would break down crying. I really struggled with how to handle seeing him that way. I realized that was not my way of handling her passing. I knew she was not really there, but that I could talk to her from wherever I was.

I briefly moved in with my aunt, my mom's sister, and my cousin to cope and heal. My dad and brother stayed in the house for a while until we made the decision to start afresh and move into a new house. I enjoyed that time with my aunt and her family, and my brother and I also spent a lot of time with both sets of grandparents as my dad had to go back to work. Every morning and every afternoon after school, my brother and I had somewhere to go. We were well taken care of.

That next summer, I picked up the tennis racquet that my mom bought me for Christmas and started to take lessons. I joined the school team and funneled my emotions and competitive spirit into becoming the best I could be in tennis. I joined a club and played multiple days a week. Tennis was my outlet. I took all my sadness and anger out on the court. Sometimes it worked in my favor and other times, I found myself frustrated and unpleasant to even be around. All of these emotions were much more than the game of tennis, of course; I just did not realize it then. I played year-round all through high school. It was my love, my passion and I always had family in the crowd cheering me on. My grandpa, in particular, never missed a practice or match. I have no doubt that even though I was not always fun to be around depending on the outcome of the game, my grandpa was there for me.

My dad was doing the best he could. He worked a high-level job and had the responsibility of taking care of two teenagers. It was not until I was in high school that he met a woman that he enjoyed spending time with. He respected us and would always go see her rather than bringing her around to our home, as he knew we would not handle that well. It was at my high school graduation party when I met her for the first time. I felt immense pain that someone other than my mom was with my father at my graduation. I knew it was selfish to think that, as she was a lovely person and seemed to make my dad happy, but I was not very accepting at first.

My time in college helped me understand my dad needed to find happiness again. He needed someone to talk to and be with outside of the relationship he had with us kids. It took me a long time to wrap my head around all of it. I had to understand that she was not trying to replace my mom; she was there for my dad and for us any time we needed her. They got engaged and were married a couple years later and are happily married to this day. We have a very strong relationship, and I appreciate the patience she has had with me, as it took me a long time to accept and embrace what she truly means to me.

Once I graduated college, I ventured out into the world of sales and spent ten years in the beer, wine, and spirit industry, slowly working my way up the corporate ladder. Any sales incentives that were up for grabs brought out my competitive nature. I had to make sure I at least did everything in my power to win. Thus, I was able to travel to amazing places, surround myself with fantastic people, and experience things that not many people get to experience. Along the way, I met my husband as he worked for the same company.

It was love at first sight for me. It may have taken him some time to come around, but when he finally did, we began to create an amazing life together. We both support each other's passions and although we may do things that the other does not always agree with, we find a way to make this life work together and laugh while we do it.

My husband was always the main breadwinner, but I wanted to contribute more to our marriage in every way. I knew I was capable. After ten years in the adult beverage industry, I was getting the itch to make a change, to challenge myself in a different way. I said yes to a corporate sales organization with an incredible culture and a supportive leadership team. I knew I could make a big impact there. I hit the ground running. My sales team was incredible, and my sales manager was more than I could ever ask for in a so-called "boss." His leadership style was empowering, motivating, and inspiring which brought out the best in me.

The one thing I received from the company and which I appreciated above all else was that they always had us focused on our "why." As a team, we needed to identify the reasons that made us get out of bed every morning. Most of my coworkers mentioned their why as being their children, family, and spouses, whereas, we never had children. My husband and I had a great marriage however, he was only a part of my "why." I knew I was striving for something bigger; I just could not pinpoint it.

The job was intense, yet it was all worth it. I had achieved the highest level of success as a sales professional—I hit President's Club. I felt like I had run a marathon mentally and emotionally at the end of my first year there. I felt relief at first, more than I felt excitement. As I sat in my backyard one evening on my 34th birthday, I thought of my mother, and reflected that she had died at the age of 34. I had this epiphany. Now that I had turned 34, all I could think was that I had so much more I wanted to accomplish, things I wanted to do and see. I had this incredible perspective. The whole world was at my fingertips and I did not want to waste a second of it. The next year was challenging. I wanted to do the exact same thing I did the year before. I wanted to hit another President's Club, but this time it felt like I was swimming upstream. I started to compare my activities and results to others. The pressure I put on myself had me more stressed than I even realized. In the spring of 2017, after a conversation with my sales manager, another opportunity presented itself. I was asked to step into a different role at a different location to gain some more experience. I wasn't overly excited about it, but I trusted my manager and knew it was for the betterment of my career, so I said yes.

On the morning of March 30th, 2017, a little more than a week later, I woke up like any other morning. I hopped in the shower and got ready for my new role. I sat on the floor to put on my socks and shoes when all of a sudden I felt extremely dizzy. I started sweating profusely, sweating right through my clothes. I knew something wasn't right so I laid down for a minute hoping these odd feelings would subside. A couple of minutes later, I called my aunt to tell her that I did not feel right and she said, "you don't sound right." I noticed that my voice started to change, and I was struggling to swallow. She told me to call 911 and promised to meet me at the hospital.

The ambulance came quickly and two EMTs calmly drove me to the nearest hospital, only ten minutes away. Upon arrival, my husband, dad, and aunt were already there. At that point, I just remember the nausea and them giving me a bucket to spit in. The doctors could not pinpoint right away what was going on. The first MRI did not show anything, so I was put into an observation room. At first, I was diagnosed with vertigo, however my family knew it was more than that. After twelve hours in the observation room and another MRI, we had our answer: I had suffered a stroke in three different areas of my brain.

When the news got out, I had a lot of visitors bringing me cards, flowers, gifts, and hugs; I felt surrounded by love. I was not able to eat anything for the first few days as the stroke had affected my ability to swallow. I was unable to walk much as I had no strength. Doctors and therapists would come in often to check vitals, do blood work, and get me to do small exercises to help with movement. My husband never left my side. He spent every night with me. I was never alone in this new unexpected chapter of my life.

After seven days in the hospital, it was time for the next step in recovery. I went to a nearby acute rehab hospital for intense physical, occupational, and speech therapy. I was taken there by ambulance and pushed to my room in a wheelchair. It never occurred to me that I was not capable of walking. I just knew that I felt overly fatigued all the time. I spent hours a day learning how to do basic things like taking a shower, reading, and walking without assistance as my balance was affected by the stroke. I had to eat a soft diet and work my way to eating normal foods without choking. I would go to support group meetings and I honestly was still not comprehending the severity of my situation.

My mother-in-law flew in from Florida and spent every day with me until my husband could come after work. I had so many friends, family, and coworkers stop by to show their love and support. Someone would spend the night with me every night and go to therapy with me every day. Overall, it was a challenging ten days, but I conquered my goals and was able to return home for the next phase in this chapter.

Outpatient rehabilitation was next for me. My friends and family were so gracious that they created a calendar for the next three months, so I knew who was taking me and picking me up every Tuesday and Thursday. Most of them stayed with me during my sessions and cheered me on. A couple of big moments stand out to me. In my reports, the therapists indicated that I had lost my left peripheral vision on day one. It was also determined that my voice was weak due to a paralyzed vocal cord, so I had to do daily exercises to regain strength. I also had to go through a lot of visual exercises and pass a driving test to retain my driver's license. My competitive nature was paying off and I was crushing all of my goals. I made awesome relationships with my therapists and still keep in touch with them to this day.

After the first twelve weeks of rehab and therapy, I went back to work. My employer was so good to me. I was able to return at my own pace. They remained patient with me and adapted to every single one of my needs. I remember being asked to speak at our annual sales meeting that summer. It was an honor to be asked to share my story with hundreds of people. I just kept thinking I did not want to get up there and cry during the talk. I wrote the speech with the help of my therapist and practiced it every day. I was able to successfully present my story with no tears. It felt crazy, but honestly, I could not even produce tears if I tried. I did not have that ability, as my brain was not able to process tears. This worked out well for me, although it was so unlike me. Before my stroke as I was always one to wear my heart on my sleeve. The response to my speech was overwhelming. It was also quite therapeutic for me.

In December of 2017, I was officially back in sales with my own territory. It was close to home and I could easily work around my doctor's appointments. The big question that still surrounded my stroke was why and how it happened. I went to several specialists over the next few months to rule out several options. I wore a heart monitor to rule out any abnormalities. I went to a hematologist where they took twenty-six vials of blood to make sure I did not have a blood disorder. They did establish that I had a high protein level which led to me seeing a couple more specialists and eventually I had thyroid surgery to keep that under control. Ultimately, no one could find the root cause of my stroke.

After the first anniversary of the stroke, there was a shift. I had physically healed the best I could. What I could not control were my emotions. I had been unable to cry before, but during a meeting with my neurologist, I cried through my entire appointment. She was ready to prescribe me something to help "keep things in control," but instead, she recommended a therapist to talk about what I was feeling. I met with two different therapists and both sessions went the same exact way: I would go in on the verge of tears already, cry throughout my entire session, and then sob all the way home. Every day, I would get through my workday, but the minute someone called me to check in, I would cry. I felt sad and depressed, but I could not explain why.

After another six months (eighteen months after my stroke) there was another shift. I was introduced to a life coach by a dear friend. I was willing to try anything. I met with the life coach and although I felt I was still an emotional disaster, there was something different about our conversations. The coach explained to me that a therapist is meant to dive into your past, uncover those issues and find a solution, where as a life coach helps you accept your present situation and teaches you how to move forward. That made a lot of sense to me. I remember her asking me during our first session if I had ever asked myself "why me?" I knew I had not necessarily done that but I was trying to figure out why things had changed so much in my life. She then asked, "why not you?" It took me a lot of time and sessions for that question to come full circle. It came back through another epiphany.

Everything was becoming clearer. When I had the stroke, I was the same age my mom was when she passed. I survived this stroke for a reason. I believe that this happened *for* me and not *to* me. I am meant to be here to honor my mom's legacy by serving others. Without the help of my life coach, I would not have come to that conclusion. She believed in me before I believed in myself. She saw more in me than I could see. We worked on several things that I needed to incorporate in my daily routine in order to switch my mindset and move past depression. One of the first things we worked on was gratitude journaling and I continue this practice to this day. It has made such a difference when I am able to reflect on my day and write down those small, simple things that made me smile.

My neurologist was determined to find the cause of my stroke and asked me to come in for additional tests. I admire her for her care and persistence and am so thankful that my medical team did not give up on me and fought to find the answers. After another CT scan, I received a call the next day saying I needed to meet her in her office. My husband met me there. The doctor informed us that she saw something concerning and wanted to do an angiogram the following morning. We drove home and I tried to sleep that night although I felt extremely anxious. The next morning, at 6:00 a.m. I went in for the procedure. My aunt and my best friend were there to hold my hand as afterwards, I had to lay flat for a couple of hours and try to remain calm. Later that morning the doctor came in with the news we had been waiting for. They had found the cause for my stroke. It was a vertebral artery dissection (VAD), a tiny tear in the back of my neck. We are still unsure how this happened. It could have been from working out, coughing, sneezing, or any number of things that could cause a sudden jarring of my neck.

The great news was they said it had scarred over and was no longer dangerous although it would need to be monitored to ensure it remains stable. The news brought me peace of mind. However, I was still bothered by emotional struggles and I found myself frustrated at the littlest things. I had no patience. I was forgetting to do things and my memory was not where it used to be. My family arranged an appointment with a neuropsychologist. My aunt met me there and we had a great conversation with the doctor. I was not sure what to expect, but I went through hours of testing with the doctor and walked out completely drained. I felt like I excelled in certain areas and failed in others. I returned a month later in hopes of answers. I received more good news. Everything was neurologically within normal range and the neuropsychologist gave me a couple suggestions to help me adapt to some of the short-term memory loss. I felt empowered as now it was up to me how I was going to overcome these challenges.

After working with my life coach for several months, I realized that one of the decisions I needed to make was to leave my current career as it was no longer fulfilling. After several conversations with upper-management, and despite how gracious they were about wanting to make accommodations so I could remain at work, I left on March 30th, 2019—my two-year stroke anniversary. I instinctively felt that I wanted to pursue something where I was going to make more of an impact on people. A friend needed someone to help her grow and market her home health business. I came on board and received a warm welcome to this locally owned and operated company where they excel at putting their patients first. I remember riding with my counterpart the first week learning the lay of the land. One of her biggest referral sources was the acute rehab I stayed at two years prior.

I was nervous yet excited to walk through the doors. She went to a patient's room to gather some information. I stood patiently until we walked out, then it hit me like a ton of bricks. That was my room. That was the room I was wheeled into, the room where I learned how to shower and make the bed, and where I had spent an intense ten days learning to do the basic things so many take for granted. We then went to meet the case manager and she immediately recognized me. She had also been my own case manager.

My experiences have led me to see that I am meant to serve others as a life coach. Everything to this point had brought me to my soul purpose, to that "why" that I struggled to identify before. I have now established my own company, Just Commit Coaching. Through certification courses, my own life experiences, and the skills I used to overcome the challenges of those experiences, I have created a program that I believe will help others. I had to realize I was not going back to my old self, but instead I had to find my new version of myself. I am here to help others discover their strengths and overcome life's challenges. I have developed a foundation that I use to guide my clients. I can wholeheartedly say it takes faith, self-care, the right mindset, gratitude, and support. I had to accept and embrace this new version of me. It also takes time and the commitment to want that for yourself. We are all a work in progress and whatever life throws at you, remember that you do have the ability to not just overcome to survive, but also remember that you were born to thrive.

We all have an unsuspected reserve of
strength inside that emerges when life puts us to the test.

ISABEL ALLENDE

PATRICIA DE PICCIOTTO

Patricia de Picciotto was born in Hong Kong, and raised in Geneva, Switzerland until she graduated from college with a BA in Marketing and Communications. She then studied in London to become a Graduate Gemologist and worked in jewelry. After a decade in Sao Paulo, Brazil, she moved to New York City in 2015 with her husband and three boys, and became an art experiences curator.

Since her mother's passing in 2019, she is now a grief coach dedicated to normalize grief through her Neshama Journey Project.

THE WOUNDED HEALER

PATRICIA DE PICCIOTTO

When a baby is born, the child feels love and warmth at first, and then goes on their own journey through life with its ups and downs, joys and pains. We aren't born wounded. The soul we carry from birth to death remains pure, if we tap into its essence. My story is filled with love and family memories, but also with abandonments and grief. I carry these wounds with me, as they have made me who I am today. Some of the wounds have remained open and my heart lovingly expanded around them. I healed by learning to live with them, care for them, and find meaning in the hardships. Our life experiences serve to transform us into the greatest version of our soul's purpose.

Saying goodbye to my mom on November 22, 2019, after her two-year pancreatic cancer battle, is the worst loss I have suffered in my life so far. Opening conversations about grief and supporting other grievers has helped me navigate my first year of mourning. Grief is a healing process. I am learning to live with an invisible scar on my heart.

ROOTS

I was born the youngest of three daughters, a decade after the birth of my eldest sibling, as my family had to relocate multiple times. My parents are of Lebanese and Syrian descent. A few years after the birth of my sisters, they had to flee Beirut, Lebanon to escape the political conflicts in the country. I couldn't understand this age gap when I was young, but my mother told me that I was a post-war baby, the one that came into the family once the dust was settled and their stability restored.

Being the baby came with advantages and disadvantages, but my birth order definitely shaped me into who I am today. I had the attention of four grown-ups but no one to play with, so I turned to my neighbors for company. I had plenty of one-on-one time with both my parents, but only until my teenage years. I had sisters to look up to but they consecutively left the house before I turned twelve to start their own families. All this might explain why I was so close to my mom, as it was me and her for as long as I can remember. From school drop offs and pick ups, to running errands, watching TV, cooking, doing homework, playing and coloring, we would be together, or rather, I would be glued to her as she would jokingly say. I was her baby until the end: that's what she told the nurse one night at the hospital before falling into unconsciousness the following morning.

THE ABANDONMENTS

I find this word to be very strong, even traumatic. It's the word I heard when I was nineteen and suffering from anxiety and a lack of perspective of what could be my future. I was finishing my second year of college, when everyone else in my family had established their own lives. At this point my oldest sister had been out of the family home since I was eight, my middle sister left when I was eleven, and my father moved to another country when I was fourteen. My parents finalized their divorce when I was fifteen. From age fourteen onward, it was me and mom, almost living like an old couple. We needed each other. She was trying her best to put on a brave face, but I knew too well the gloom that was behind her smiles. My father leaving was an absence that weighed on both of us, on me more that I could fathom at that time. The heartache showed up in me physically years later. It took me until I was mature enough to understand where that pain came from so I could take care of it and eliminate it.

I gifted my mom the CD, "I Will Survive" by Gloria Gaynor, and survived we did. Weeknights we would watch TV and fall asleep in her bed, not questioning if it was wrong or right to have a teenage girl sleeping with her mother because it felt good for both of us to have each other's company, especially in the evenings when everything can seem lonelier. After a couple of years, I had a boyfriend and I would talk on the phone to him at bedtime, so I started sleeping in my own bedroom more frequently. I was also going out a lot more on weekends. I felt like I was abandoning my mom in a way, but I think she was relieved to have some time for herself and happy to see me having some normal teenage experiences.

Then in 2001, my mother met a Brazilian man and relocated with him, the following year moving to the other side of the ocean leaving me all alone in our family apartment in Geneva, Switzerland. Where we used to be a family of five now it was just me. Moving out of the house to get married, as they all did, one after the other over a decade, is not legally considered abandonment but emotionally it was for me. As much as I was relieved and happy that my mother found love again and was moving on with her life, I could not help but experience the compounded pain of her leaving.

That summer is one of my unhappy memories. I remember crying a lot and feeling lonely, until I looked for professional help. Halfway through our first session, the therapist said: "you feel like an abandoned little girl!" He had put words to that feeling of emptiness. From then on, I had to rebuild myself with self-love and understand that I would never be alone in my own company.

THE MISDIAGNOSIS

The following experience shaped my future and my views on how body, mind, soul, and life events are greatly intertwined and can make an impact on one's health, either positively or negatively. My parents' divorce, when I was a teenager and the only child living at home at that time, affected me considerably. Of course, I was sad. I missed my father a lot and was angry that the family was now reduced to two under the same roof. I was envious of the picture in my imagination of a traditional family life I would not be able to get. One with mommy and daddy home together and siblings around to play and grow up with. At that point I had many nieces and nephews, but they were all much younger than me and not living with us. As much as we tried to see them often, at home it was mom and I. We became closer and closer every day, with the occasional mother-daughter fight. We bonded over the fact that we had each other to confide to, and as a thank you gift to her trust in me, I only rarely gave her reasons to worry about my behavior.

I would often worry about our future, my mother, now a middle-aged divorcee with me as her sole roommate. This was mixed with resentment towards my father. I didn't know at the time that these emotions were damaging my body. Not aware of the influence of the mind and unexpressed feelings on one's mental and physical health, I went to see a doctor at the age of seventeen, for some unsupportable digestive problems. This physician, a luminary in the gastroenterology world, took a brief look at me, without any examination or request for further test, and concluded, based on a few questions about my lifestyle, that my stomach aches were caused by school stress. A young seventeen-year-old, whose parents had recently separated, in her last year of high school preparing for college, in his eyes, couldn't be taken seriously. He prescribed me an anti-depressant, without any psychological evaluation or a deeper look into my physical condition. His patronizing decision left me misdiagnosed. I had to endure the discomfort for three years before I found the right doctor who identified the causes of my suffering.

1999-2002 DEALING WITH MY HEALTH

Leaving my teen years was not without its challenges, but I was not going to enter a new decade without putting up a fight. I turned nineteen in 2001 and was really down until I realized, by some fruitful and sometimes random encounters, that I had my future in my hands. I was the only one responsible for it. I understood that it was ok not to be a sheep and follow the herd on a path that was destined for me. I could wander around to see what else I could achieve.

I had entered my third year of college and switched my major from economy to marketing and communication, realizing that walking in my father's footsteps to work in finance was not at all what I wanted for my career. I could be what I chose to be, not what I was expected to be. I was still living at home with my mom although she already had one foot in Brazil with her future husband. I had a part-time job at a magazine as a junior editor in the lifestyle section and it brought me much joy to write about my discoveries. Unfortunately, I was still affected by terrible digestive issues that had worsened and were now impacting my mood and disposition.

I had returned to that infamous doctor who, again, without any medical exams but just based on my age and narration, switched the anti-depressants to irritable colon syndrome prescription. Nothing was helping so I took the matter in my own hands. As it was the time when Google was too recent to auto diagnose you, I did my research in books and magazines on alternative therapies. This was the first step to healing. I became determined to be an active participant in my cure and realized that whatever was causing me the physical discomfort started with and within me, so I had to make the change happen. This is a lesson I still apply to this day. Of course, doctors are needed, but they are not the sole responsible and savior of one's health. I decided to experiment with other methods: acupuncture, osteopathy, energy healing, homeopathy, and naturopathy... it definitely helped me, especially in feeling that I was proactive about my health, and not apathetic about the situation. But the apathy had lodged already in my body, and everything I was undergoing would not be able to reverse the damages that were done, probably by the sadness, anger, and resentment that still nested within my body.

The summer of my twenties, my mom, who had been a pillar and a constant support in my life for two decades, moved with all her luggage to São Paulo. I visited her once she was settled, and I was comforted that she had started a new life in a place where she immediately felt welcome. Leaving her and going back alone to Geneva wasn't easy on my heart. A part of me wanted to be independent, to live on my own, to party at home, to be responsible for everything: I became the captain of my own ship, but I was losing my safe harbor. Both my parents were established so far away from me.

2002-2003 THE HEALING CAN START

I still remember the day when I was crying and begging our family doctor to find me other specialists, a new gynecologist and a new gastroenterologist. My health situation took a turn for the worst, although I got better at managing the pain with all the different therapies I was using. But something was still wrong, totally off: this is not how a healthy-looking twenty-year-old should feel. Just by physical examination and some tests (as simple as it sounds although it had not been performed by the previous infamous doctor), they were able to discover what was bothering me and exactly why my symptoms had worsened in the past four years. I had a hernia in my colon that had grown as big as a tennis ball, causing my digestive problems and a general loss in muscle strength in multiple organs. This untreated hernia grew out of proportion, causing me even more pain and sadness that ended up shutting down my intestines, ovaries, uterus, and bladder. I used to be so embarrassed explaining the symptoms, and although I am much more comfortable now that they are gone, it was not very glamorous to discuss bowel movements, incontinence, and amenorrhea (loss of periods) in my twenties. I will never forget the look of compassion in the teary eyes of my new physician when he announced that this part of my body was like that of an elderly woman, and that I would need reconstructive surgery and a couple of years of physiotherapy to recover all the muscles and functions in the area. As bad as the news was, once again, having someone put words to my pain was the beginning of healing.

MY FIRST JOURNEY TO HEALING FORGIVENESS

Although my focus was on my healing process, I instinctively knew that the physical difficulties were coming from a deeper issue, not just anatomical ones. Why would a young woman, in overall good health, have organs slowing down to that point? I had the surgery in 2003 and started intensive physiotherapy, that I would endure for another two years. I also included acupuncture, energy healing, and reiki. The surgeon and physiotherapist would help repair the mechanical problems but in my mind I had more that needed to be fixed.

At that moment, although I wasn't looking for anything in partic-ular, two books caught my attention: *Heal Your Body and The Power is Within You* from Louise Hay, author of several self-help books. Louise Hay believed one's mind influences the body. Consequently, one's attitudes and experiences a well as sadness, resentment, anger, or other negative emotions and beliefs can affect your health, not only on a mental but also on a physical level. She advocated for positive mindset and affirmations: the healing power within us that only we can control and decide to change.

Subsequently, I had a striking and unforgettable occurrence that happened to me during a reiki session. Just like when I was ready to encounter these books, my soul was open for what was coming next: as soon as my reiki master put his hands on my face to cover my eyes, after muttering some prayers, I felt a rush of energy being pushed from my feet to the top of my head. Something inexplicable struck me at that moment. I felt it all through my body and I suddenly burst into an uncontrollable sob that probably lasted the entire session. You know how some people have reported that they see their whole life flash in front of their eyes when they were about to die? Well right after the ethereal shock, I started seeing image after image of memories with my father, from my childhood until that present time. Exhausted by the spiritual discharge, I knew it could mean only one thing: forgiveness.

I had shed many tears before, but this was not a simple cry, it was an emotional cleanse. I needed to let go of the past. I had let that sadness lodge into my body for too many years already. Acknowledging what happened in the past isn't condoning it but accepting it so that we can forgive. This was the first step on this journey of healing, and an important tool I would need to heal what I will feel was the biggest abandonment of all, the death of my mother.

FIGHTS AND HOPES

When my mother was diagnosed with pancreatic cancer, on January 12, 2018, nothing could have prepared me for it. I had gone to a party the night before, a million years from imagining that the next day I would wake up to that traumatic text message my oldest sister sent me. Due to the time zone difference, it was still very early in New York, where I had relocated. After a dozen missed calls, my sister decided to write me the devastating news so I would call them back immediately.

I was in shock. It felt like everything was falling apart and I couldn't stop crying, even when I was on the phone with my mother. I had not recovered from the news a month prior, that my stepfather's cancer was not treatable anymore and he had only a few months... and now this! Pancreatic cancer sounds like a death sentence, and over ninety percent of the time it is, but the surgeon was confident that the tumor could be removed, and that chemo would kill the rest of the cells. He was right, and for six months my mother went on her first fight against the disease, but once in remission, her husband passed away. She received the remission news when he was in his final days and she had her last chemo the week she was "sitting shivah" for him (a Jewish ritual of mourning with prayers and visits from the community, going on for a week after the passing).

Grief and sadness overwhelmed her, and loneliness hit her as well. For as bad as the last months were, taking care of him and undergoing chemo herself, they were still together. Sometimes, even a harsh situation is sweeter than total emptiness. I felt the same when she died after months in hospital: it was better to be by her bedside, even in terrible conditions, than without her at all.

After she passed, I hated when people would serve platitudes like, "she is resting now," "she is not suffering anymore," "she is in a better place." But why did she need to suffer anyway? I wanted to shout back. And who said it's better now? Having little conversations in a hospital room is better than total silence, isn't it? Taking care of someone's suffering is still a demonstration of love and is better than no interaction at all…

ANTICIPATORY GRIEF

Anticipatory grief is a bitch! Excuse my French but it's true… My mom and her husband lived in denial for six months until his passing, but I came to realize that they were both trying to protect each other: she didn't want to remind him that he was dying (which I am sure he could not forget) and he wanted her to focus on her treatment. They hadn't discussed anything about their feelings and wishes or the life after. I begged my mom, when he was unconscious to tell him all she had on her heart, that she will be ok, and that he could rest now. She felt awkward to do so and said that talking about death before someone is actually dead, is like condemning him. At that moment it was his fate anyway and no superstition could change it.

My anticipatory grief went differently: when my mother's cancer came back and six months later, they found metastasis in her liver, I knew in my heart she was sentenced, but we all kept our hopes high. She underwent a last possible treatment that took a turn to the worst, plunging her immunity to its lowest levels and leaving her body vulnerable to infections. In her final three months of life, she spent two months hospitalized and one at home, still hopeful that this time she would recover. Looking back, we must have been delusional as the chances were so low and she had been so weak. Hope is the last to die. It was shattered when her oncologist asked to talk to me alone outside of her hospital room and told me to call the family now. He could not even tell me if her death would come in days or weeks.

I was devastated by the news and still had to make those phone calls. The following three weeks were like a dark cloud of death lingering above us. Every time I left her whether just momentarily, I did not know if she would be there when I returned or wake up in the morning. I started looking for grief books and podcasts, even shopping online for the black dress I knew I would soon need and didn't bring with me. A selfish part of me wanted to keep her alive, even though she was suffering but another prayed for this painful situation to end. I wanted her to rest in peace, but not forever, and not so soon.

THE LOSS

My mom died five days after her seventieth birthday that she fought so hard to witness and celebrate with close family and friends. She wanted to be present at her farewell party and fell unconscious only two days later. She taught me everything but not how to live without her. The day she died I lost my first love, my best friend, my safety net, my role model in motherhood, and my biggest supporter. My world was shattered: a piece of me died with her but so much of her lives in me forever. When I realized this, I was able to accept her death and understand that I will grieve her as long as she is gone, and I will honor her values, legacy, and teachings as long as I breathe.

THE PAUSE

Mourning is the public demonstration and rituals of grief… it ends. Grief is what you carry in your heart, forever. To follow my mother's religious tradition, I mourned for a year within the Jewish faith rules. Not only is it a pause in time, but it also stripped me from all the social, material, and superficial aspects of life and required that

I focus on the spiritual side and on my grief. It seems incongruous at first, but it helped me tremendously. For a year I didn't go to parties or social gatherings, buy new clothes or glam myself up. I didn't want to do any of these anyway, and these rules just gave me a dignified reason to say no, to stay home, and to avoid people and unbearable small talk. Suddenly this became the norm, as the world faced a pandemic and lockdowns started just four months into my first year of grief. As devastating as COVID-19 was on a human and economic scale, I was able to find blessings in this pause. I needed to stay home, sit with myself and honor my feelings.

Grief is very isolating and the phone stops ringing too early. Being in quarantine an ocean away from my family, made me feel even lonelier. I thought I was alone, but I wasn't. There was an online grief community out there that I didn't know existed. People were talking about their losses and grief, their sadness and longing. They were sharing experiences and most importantly, giving space to other grievers.

All I had been through earlier in life was within me, and at that moment it all came back to me that I healed my wounds once and I could do it again. My mother always listened and cared for others and in finding meaning in her life's teachings, I will give my support to other grievers and shed light on a taboo subject in our grief-illiterate society. Home for months and also paused from my job as an art guide, I created an account on Instagram, Neshama Journey (soul in Hebrew), to open the conversation and give other grievers a chance to share their stories, as one's experience can always be an example for others. My mom's soul is on her journey in what I believe is the afterlife, and mine is still on her journey here, but they are forever linked.

By talking about my mom and my grief vulnerably, I was healing myself, helping others, and honoring her legacy. We die twice, first when we're gone and second when no one talks about us anymore, so I made it my mission to keep her memory alive.

THE HEALING GRIEF PROCESS

In the grief healing process, there are many shades of grief and nuances of pain. It isn't straightforward. There is a gray area where wounded people heal by learning to live with this incurable wound. There is no treatment for it, but it can be mended by dressing it with love and finding a purpose, which for me is healing with, and through, others.

There is no darkness without light, and I believe light came before darkness, in life too. If there is no love, there is no grief, and it's that love that makes us suffer for the loss but that also helps us overcome it too. I was brave enough to face the hardships I encountered throughout my life because I had been loved and collected cherished memories that brought me so much gratitude when I thought there was nothing to be grateful for. They were somewhere in my heart and soul, and by feeling it all without trying to numb it, they came back to the surface so I could recover. Grief changes a person forever, but in going through the process you will be able to find meaning in the life, values, and experiences you shared with your loved ones.

We hear that time heals everything... No, time changes it. It makes it different, and maybe less intense. The healer is in us, it always is, but I agree that it requires time, clarity, and willingness to find the healer and the cure within. We give sense to our pains by the way we react to them. We can't control them, but we can control by which attitude we choose to face them. We can embrace and share our journey to help ourselves and others. It is through expressing our pain rather than hiding it, that we can understand that each of us have soul lessons to learn through our human experience.

It was the year 2020 that I rebuilt myself after my world had been shattered. It was a year that will also mark humankind forever and made history by all the death and downfalls around the world. The pandemic left us with wreckage, losses, perspective, and the understanding of what truly matters in life; a focus on what is essential. Hopefully, humanity on this grieving journey will come together to mourn, heal, and create a collective consciousness: a soul connection to one another to help us find our true purpose.

How could I have known that the death of one person could be the rebirth of another one? I never thought my mother would give birth to me twice, the day I was born and then the day she died. Because of my grief journey, I have found my soul purpose and have transformed into the woman I am today. I want to learn, heal, teach, encourage, support, and empower other grieving hearts by being of service to them. I will continue to create a safe space and encourage others to share their stories, voice their pain, and help them realize they are not alone. From our deepest wounds come our greatest ability to heal. That's the life lesson of the wounded healer.

Nobody escapes being wounded. We are all wounded people, whether physically, emotionally, mentally, or spiritually. The main question is not, 'How can we hide our wounds?' so we don't have to be embarrassed, but 'How can we put our woundedness in the service of others?' When our wounds cease to be a source of shame, and become a source of healing, we have become wounded healers.

HENRI NOUWEN

HEATHER DI SANTO

Heather believes that everything that happens in life is unexpected, but precise. Embracing her spiritual journey led her to this perspective and place of calm. She is on a mission to educate leaders by using innovative tools and training for personal and professional development through powerful conversations and workshops. She is passionate about facilitating dynamically integrated soul healing event experiences as the powerhouse entrepreneur behind DiSH Events, whose core values are community, collaboration, and connection.

THE LETTER

HEATHER DI SANTO

*You begin to fly when you let go of self-limiting
beliefs and allow your mind and
aspirations to rise to greater heights.*

BRIAN TRACY

Dear Heather,

Love, laughter, faith, sleep, and life.

You own them all—everyone.

They will carry you along your road in life towards your goal.

You will learn that success is measured not so much by the position
you have reached in life as the obstacles which you have overcome
while trying to succeed.

This is a new year. For some it will be cold and lonely but for you
searching for a new horizon you will find happiness.

Do not make your life a hundred yards.

Life has so much to give,
for you will find there is a kind of race you ought to live.

Just make your life a relay race.

Where others run with you,
you start, another takes the pace you set, and carries through.

For life is not a hundred yards,
a dash or a marathon.

The best race run is where each one has helped his team along the way.

No day is ever wasted if you have a happy song in even one heart
somewhere. Because you came along, each day is an opportunity.
So, use it, every minute, and make the world a nicer place, because
it has you in it.

Love and love always.
Good luck! Nana

I was in the fortieth year of my life when I was given this letter. It was the day of my nana's funeral. I believe that a person has two births: the day you were born and the day you discover why. This letter led to my second birth.

I was still in my corporate career at the time of her death, and I was sad. Being a busy careerwoman, a wife, and a mother of two young boys, I had made little time to visit my nana in the last few years of her life. My priorities were messed up and I spent more time working than enjoying my life. I was so wrapped up in the *doing* of life, following a path that served me well, but it was also one that I never completely felt whole in. I was considered successful but never felt the same way about myself as others saw me. Prior to her dementia, I had told my nana many times that I wasn't doing the work I wanted to do for the rest of my life. That I felt there was something more for me, but I was living with a belief that having a job and security was more important than going after my dreams.

I understand that it may seem strange, but when I received this letter, it sparked something inside of me. It lit a fire that from that moment forward I knew things had to be different. I felt like I had been touched by God through my nana. I now know that it's when my self-worth development journey began. It gave me purpose to explore my world a little differently. It explained why I always wanted to learn more about myself, and why I ticked the way I did. It sparked a feeling that I could do more and be more than what I was at the time.

My nana saw me. She really knew me; I just hadn't realized it. What a wonderful aha moment. The transformation didn't happen overnight, but I believe receiving this letter was the catalyst for changing my perspective, my reality, and the trajectory of my future.

THE GOOD GIRL

For as long as I can remember, I have woken up in the morning with a fluttering feeling in the pit of my stomach. It is best described as butterflies but my association with it is nowhere near sunshine and rainbows. I don't remember when it began. It doesn't just happen in the morning, but I notice it several times a day. I have become aware now that it happens when I'm about to do something that's out of my comfort zone, or when I feel guilty about something, and even while I am ruminating about situations. So, yes, it happens a lot, come to think of it.

I am a woman with a zest for life and the people in it. I love movement and my family. I am a dedicated wife and mother and a well-liked, successful event planner and entrepreneur. Yet, with all this awesomeness, I am also a woman who lives with a shadow that's weighed her down for forty-five years. It is the feeling of anxiety, fear, and a long list of limiting beliefs. My brain swirls with mind-bending thoughts of not being good enough. I care too much about what others think of me. I have constant worry which fills my entire being with thoughts of what I will be scared to do or not do that day. This, as I describe it, is *analysis paralysis* which makes me hesitate to move anything forward without being certain of the outcome.

I don't recall a particular pivotal event where fear and numerous limiting beliefs were instilled in me. I believe it has been a series of experiences and perceptions that created layers of complex and awful things I thought about myself. These are thoughts I have never shared because from the outside looking in, I had and have everything and more. I have always been respected with numerous friends surrounding me. I am a perfectionist and a rule follower, who has done everything in her power to be seen, heard, understood, and loved.

I have also always perceived myself as a good girl. Growing up, it was integral for me to be proper, well-mannered, and I strove, dangerously perhaps, to appear to be perfect. I knew as a young girl when I was out of line; my mom would shoot me a look if I was doing something inappropriate, in her opinion. For punishment, I was told to sit quietly on a chair by myself in a room, but in ear shot of where my mom was preparing dinner that had to be on the table when my dad got home from work. I would have to sit and think about what I did wrong, how I was going to make it right, and apologize for whatever I'd done. I remember sometimes sitting for what felt like hours because I felt I'd done nothing wrong. Feeling sick to my stomach with confusion for why my perception of the incident warranted the punishment. I believe it shaped feelings of isolation and invisibility, feeling not good enough, and a resistance to using my voice until my response was perfect enough so I could move again and make my mom happy. I have always felt like my family's happiness revolved around me.

Throughout my entire life, it has been so important to me to make Nana and my parents proud of me. I worked hard at that and my worth was wrapped around their approval of me and what I did in my life.

THE ONLY CHILD

My mom loves to mention that as a little girl I was always considered to be friendly, approachable, well-known, and liked. "Oh! You're Heather's dad! She's such a delight!" My mom relays the story gleefully, and apparently, when my dad would arrive at functions at school, church, and extra curriculars this is what strangers would often say to him. Mom would always tell me that it made my dad extremely proud.

Truth be told, I can always remember wanting to have people around me yet never feeling like I completely belonged. A square peg in a round hole around others but wonderfully comfortable being by

VOICES

myself. Being an only child it's a bit of a requirement to be able to stand by yourself. I suppose. I like to say that I'm an *introverted extrovert*. That best describes how I've always worked in the world. I love to be with people and when the party is over, my safe place is in the quiet of my home, with my thoughts. As I've put the pieces together, it has also provided some clarity as to where my anxiety came from.

I remember being told once that my dad wanted a boy. Whether that happened or not, I'm not entirely sure, but looking back on some old photos from my early childhood, I think I'd agree based on the way I was dressed! That phase seemed to have quickly passed as I moved into wearing dresses and appeared as a girly-girl in public. My dad loved to shop, and it became "our thing." In the summer, he loved to take me to buy my clothes for back-to-school. Throughout my childhood, shopping was a momentous occasion, and I loved every minute of it. In fact, shopping was always a bonding experience for my family. Having "things" was important to us. As did matching from head to toe and being picture perfect. The weight of the responsibility I felt to be perfect and to make my parents happy and proud was very heavy.

Our vacations were always planned around trips to outlet malls. We would spend our Christmases in Florida visiting my nana, where as a family we'd head off to the mall. If my dad found a shirt he liked and found it to be reasonably priced, he'd buy every color. He would go to all the stores with petite sizes and seek out what he thought would look best on my mom. Her and I would typically shop together and when we met at our pre-determined time, he'd say, "come with me" and off they'd go, and she'd purchase the best outfits for the "best price." These are some of my fondest memories of family time and solidified the definition of abundance in my mind. Abundance equated to money; money bought things, which in turn, made us happy.

We spent summers at the cottage, and I remember it being some of the best and carefree moments of my life. I don't recall having any fear of doing any kind of activities, especially when I was by myself. Being alone felt safe and a place where I didn't have to prove myself to anyone. At home, I would spend hours in our basement playing teacher. I would have my stuffed animals in chairs around the blackboard as I would stand and facilitate the lesson to them.

What sticks out for me is the polarity of the comfort I felt as a child with being myself and fearless, and how that changed as I grew up. I had forgotten the child within and conformed to what others thought I should do and should be. Being alone and with my thoughts gave me time to analyze every little moment of my life. I felt guilty for the ease of life that I had. I spent my life making decisions so that my parents and those around me were happy. To me, that meant I was deserving of their love, support, and recognition. Those choices, I believe, contributed to my anxiety, people pleasing tendencies, limiting beliefs, fear of change, and always wanting to do more for others than myself.

To this day, I wonder if anyone in my family was genuinely happy. I may have digested all the things my mom said to herself under her breath, like "you're so stupid." I must have thought it to be true because I say it to myself now in moments when I've done something careless. I've been perpetuating this word in my head that's created fear, perceived failures, and feelings of unworthiness.

I rarely had the feeling that I was as deserving of the perceived successes and accomplishments I have had in life.

THE CORPORATE GRIND

I met my husband the summer before I was to return to my third year of college. I was a summer student, and he was working full-time before he planned to go back to school. That was one of the most fun summers of my life and at the end there was no way I was going to leave town. It was the first time in years I had felt love again and knew it felt right. Making that decision led to our marriage, two sons, an eighteen-year corporate career, and a wonderful family life. In my work life, I was considered successful, but I never felt satisfied or like I was making a difference.

I had a series of jobs over many years, and I was making money. There was a sense of security that I always had growing up. Naturally, I chose to follow in my dad's footsteps, got comfortable, and was considered successful with everything I did. This was important for me because I had so much guilt for disappointing my dad. I don't know for sure if I actually disappointed him, or if it was my perception. A corporate career equated to success and everyone was happy, except for me.

What I recall most about this chapter in my life was the constant search for who I was. I would write on every resume—"on a continuous search for knowledge and personal growth opportunities." And when I landed a great job at the bank, I took every opportunity the bank provided to take courses to learn about myself. Every opportunity to escape from the work and detach from the responsibilities I didn't feel worthy of. I constantly felt stagnant sitting behind my desk. I loved to network, get to know people, engage in conversation, and see things from other's perspectives. I remember always telling people I wanted more.

Over time, I had built a community where I felt safe and respected. I was dedicated to the work which equated to a paycheck. I lived that mindset, knowing that it really wasn't what I was supposed to be doing. I didn't know how to listen to myself and trust my instincts. I spent years in positions because I was comfortable and made many choices for the betterment of others.

Much of the work I did, others got the credit for. During the last few years, I was surrounded by people who were as miserable as I was but didn't know there was a better way. I remember feeling so emotionally drained every day but also wanting to find the light in every situation. I always tried to make others look and feel better and obtain more. Everything had to appear perfect. This all happened at the expense of my happiness, freedom, and creativity. I knew my life had more meaning and more purpose. I desired more, but from where? How?

THE LETTER

I remember getting the letter from my nana like it was yesterday. Reading it gave me a profound sense of worthiness and an understanding that there was more to life left for me to live. A knowing grew in me that aligned exactly with how I was feeling at the time. The letter wasn't dated, and I remember wondering when she'd written it because she had suffered with dementia for years before her death. This letter was a calling to me and her final way of telling me that she thought I was worthy, wonderful, and capable. That I was meant for bigger things here on this Earth. Funny enough, they were all the things she had told me while I was growing up, but never believed.

The letter got me thinking about making a significant change. It was so scary for me to even think about leaving the security and money the corporate world offered; however, I felt very passionately that this was my time. Many people thought I was crazy but at the time my dream job had been manifested and there was no turning back. I recall my dad being especially proud of me and extremely worried about the financial implication of my choice. Nevertheless, he was my steadfast cheerleader and for the first time I was proud of myself for stepping out of my comfort zone.

THE JOB

I started a new job in October 2015; I was so excited for the year ahead, but with no actual comprehension of what was in store for me. I could write a whole other chapter with stories from the most inspirational, almost deadly, rewarding, impactful, hilarious, and painful experiences I had that year. One I will never forget: After executing twenty-two events in five months and barely seeing my family, I had accomplished one of the biggest feats of my life but was burnt out beyond belief.

My boss and I rarely saw eye to eye on things. That entire year was him trying to get me to work his way. Our communication was challenged, and it caused a lot of tension between us. The irony is never lost on me that we were raising money for women's mental health and yet mine was the worst it had ever been. I never stood up for myself because I was too scared to use my voice. I kept telling myself, "this is what you signed up for. This was supposed to be your dream job!" Again, I knew in my gut that this was not the best fit for me, my boss, our team, or my family, but I was not about to quit.

I was blindsided when I was fired. The reason: "not a good fit." Despite knowing that it was true, what I heard and digested was that I wasn't good enough. I had taken a chance, embraced fear, and failed. It validated all the limiting beliefs I'd had my entire life.

Going on unemployment was devastating to me. I knew deep down that finally it was my time to try things on my own. I knew that I had to "get over" myself. As terrifying as it was, I felt that the timing was right.

THE VISION BOARD

I was invited to do a vision board workshop around this time. Having never been to one before, it seemed to be the "entrepreneurial thing to do" at the beginning of a year. I remember not having much vision for what my business was going to look like and found myself cutting out and pasting inspirational words and sayings. A lot of them. And none of them aligned with how I felt about myself at the time but I knew they were what I needed to keep moving forward.

In the middle of the vision board was the saying, "Live the life you love. Love the life you live" by Bob Marley, surrounded by others like:

Choose your own path.
It always seems impossible until it's done.
Believe.
Let go.
You've got this.
Inspire.

Focus.
Balance.
Organize.
Freedom.
Do Good. Feel Good.

I was so proud of this piece of art. I hung it on a wall in my bedroom and would walk past it every day for many years, years that I had spent starting and working my own business but tiptoeing around and oftentimes standing right outside my comfort zone. I created and surrounded myself with a community of likeminded business owners who saw me for the real me. Perfectly imperfect. They were with me as I cultivated and maintained friendships, enjoyed my family, and had fun along the way.

I embraced spirituality, a word that I don't even think I knew the definition of during my corporate years. Through this exploration I have learned more about myself than I could have ever imagined. I've learned to trust the journey and that we are here for a reason. I've read countless books on self-love, self-worth and overcoming those limiting beliefs that have crippled me. I've taken a self-image course to shift the negative perceptions I'd lived with for so long to positive words of affirmation.

Through my business I help people achieve their own happiness and growth. I have tools that have helped me transform my thoughts, beliefs, habits, and perceptions. All of these experiences have had an impact on the way I feel about myself and the world around me.

During this time, my dad was diagnosed with dementia. It brought up memories of my nana's journey and again I found myself sad. I was happy that I had the freedom to support my family through this next phase, but I remember feeling like it was another fork in the road of my moving forward. I went looking for my nana's letter to gain inspiration and I couldn't find it anywhere. I was devastated. The guilt and shame washed over me. How could I be so irresponsible to have misplaced such a valuable piece of my story? I remember feeling like a complete disappointment and very angry with myself for not taking better care. For years I carried that guilt inside of me and I had even forgotten what the letter said.

THE DAYS I WILL NEVER FORGET

My dad would often, and several times in a visit, ask me what I was doing now. He remembered I had left the bank but never understood the success and contentment I have found as an entrepreneur. I felt sad and angry that it had taken me so long to find my true self and when I did it was too late to share my joy with him. However, a friend told me it wasn't too late and that he could still hear me. I was blessed to be able to talk to him about everything those last few days of his life.

I told him what I was doing and that I had an amazing community all around me supporting me. I told him that he was such an amazing dad, did a good job raising me and that I loved him. I mentioned that I would never consider myself to be a disappointment again and that he would be so proud. I played his favorite music and I have never felt so connected to someone as I did with him in those days. I reassured him repeatedly that our family and I were okay, and that my husband would take care of my mom and me. As I placed my children's pictures on his heart, I told him that his grandsons (his pride and joy) would miss him terribly.

My favorite memory will be the conversation I had with one of his nurses when she came to drop off his freshly washed clothes. Knowing he was never going to wear them again, as she placed them gently in the closet, she remarked on how many clothes he had. I laughed out loud and proceeded to tell her about our love of shopping and how it was my dad's mission in life to make sure we all were wearing the "best of the best" in clothes. As I told the story, my dad, who was non-responsive by that point made out the smallest smile from the corner of his mouth.

My dad's death was soul-changing to me. The gift of spending those last days with him will forever remind me of the gift of life. I felt the hand of God with us the entire time, and I know he chose to die holding my husband's hand after being told he would take care of us.

THE BUTTERFLY

Since my dad's death, everything has been different. I have a new sense of purpose to fulfill my dreams, continue to pursue my passions, and to live life to its fullest to honor my dad. I know he will watch me from above and continue to be proud of me. This time, I am certain he is proud.

The Universe provides when you most need it. Feeling lost in the death of my dad I thought again of the letter my nana wrote to me so long ago. As a family we shared with joy our thoughts on how they would be reunited in heaven and be our guardian angels.

One day, I had a conversation with a friend about writing this chapter and how scared I was about telling my story for fear of throwing my parents under the bus for the ways I interpreted their love and support all my life. I returned from a walk and felt called to look for journals I wrote as a teenager. Maybe they would give me the inspiration I needed. I walked over to the bookshelf where I thought they were. In front of the bookshelf was the vision board that had recently moved from my bedroom to my office after four years of it being in the same place. As I placed my hand on the vision board to move it forward to find my journals, I felt something on the back of it. I looked down and saw the manilla envelope that I knew was the missing letter from my nana.

To this day, I find it hard to describe the reaction I had when I pulled off the envelope I had clearly taped to the back of the vision board years before. I hugged it. I cried. I laughed. I shrilled. I said thank you repeatedly. In that moment there was clarity that everything up until that moment happened for a reason. That looking at the vision board of inspirational words and sayings for all those years had slowly transformed me inside and out. In that moment of pure elation, I looked up and out the window of my office and saw two doves perched on the lamppost across the street, directly in my view. This sign and its meaning were layers and pieces of the puzzle I've needed to overcome the feelings I've had in my stomach all these years. I perceived it as excitement versus fear. Joy versus worry. Determination versus anxiety. That all along, but especially now, I was being guided, loved, and supported from above. I have the validation that I have "got this" and could let go. That my journey, all the beauty and pain that comes with it, has the next phase. Oh, my nana knew the "true me" all along.

After she died, every time I would see a monarch butterfly I would say, "Hi, Nana" and I felt her presence. As I wrote this story, an awareness came flooding over me. The timing of my nana's death and that the fact that the letter that was "missing" during the most transformational years of my life, only to find it after my dad's passing, tells me for certain that I've been on the right path all along. I know that my bravery and courage in leaving behind negative thought patterns and influences has transformed my life. I will continue to move forward and focus on what's important to me and what feels right. At some point, my future self will reflect again on the person that I am today. My mission is to make myself proud by staying authentically me, and above all, believing in myself.

We delight in the beauty of the butterfly,
but rarely admit the changes it has
gone through to achieve that beauty.

MAYA ANGELOU

Sometimes you don't realize
your own strength
until you come face to face
with your greatest weakness.

SUSAN GALE

BRI DIMIT

Bri Dimit is an inspiring force of love and brilliance determined to spread light wherever she goes. As a Storytelling Musician and Keynote Speaker, she believes everyone has a story that matters. As an expert at resilience and turning life's challenges into celebrations, Bri uses her creativity to help others with their stories by amplifying the voices of others through her music. Bri is one badass businesswoman.

FIND YOUR WAY

BRI DIMIT

You will find a way.
Don't listen to what they say.
Find a way.

Growing up with constant change, adapting to new people and surroundings was considered normal for my family. Every four to five years of my life we uprooted and moved due to the nature of my dad's job. He was a college baseball coach. It was common for a contract to last about that long and because of his success and passion for coaching, he would always have a great final season and get a new offer, ultimately resulting in another family move. This lifestyle made our family close. My mom was a schoolteacher and she was always involved in our extracurricular activities. This helped the new environments always feel like home. My sister and I leaned on each other quite a bit and were best friends. Family baseball games were some of our most cherished memories and we all essentially became each other's fans.

At the age of five I was diagnosed with epilepsy, a neurological condition associated with irregular electrical activity impacting the brain. Because of this, I struggled cognitively, mentally, socially, and physically. As a child, feeling like I would never keep up with my peers became more natural than brushing my teeth every morning. Comparison got the best of me and I felt that I was never enough. I just wanted to be "normal" but all I felt was different. School was hard, friends were hard, sports were hard. You get it. Verbal communication and expression were particularly difficult for me, so I found it easier to put my thoughts on paper. This led me to tap into my creative side. I wrote journal entries but also songs, poems, and lyrics to cope.

I missed a lot of school to attend regular neurology appointments, experienced multiple electroencephalograms (EEGs), trialed multiple medications, and at one point, I was prescribed twenty pills a day. Ten in the morning, ten at night. Epilepsy is treatable but not curable and we honestly tried everything.

By age ten I was having about three to seven seizures a day. It essentially became a routine for our family, but one morning I woke up feeling worse than usual. I ended up having a "grand mal" seizure that lasted over five minutes long resulting in a 911 call. When the ambulance arrived, I was still having the seizure. Realizing this was far more serious than any of us, including the doctors, thought, I was air lifted to a children's hospital where I flatlined and was pronounced dead.

FIND A WAY.

A few minutes later I awoke. Doctors weren't sure how or why. I just woke up. To be honest, I can hardly even remember the experience except for the stories I have heard my family share. This is because every time I have a seizure, I experience memory loss and I am unable to remember what had just happened. It is a hard reality, but especially during that particular experience. What if I just met God? Who would forget that?

As you can imagine, this particular experience only made me struggle even more, especially academically. So much so, that each of the three schools I attended that year, asked me to leave. Each school gave a different excuse but all amounted to the same end result. "Unfortunately, we cannot provide the services your child needs." "There is nothing more we can do." "She is just different." After countless days of me coming home from school in tears trying my "damndest" to keep up, my mom, who was a licensed teacher, finally said, "enough" and decided to homeschool me.

Because of the irregular activity in my brain, traditional learning through worksheets and timed tests had not worked. It never clicked. So, when my mom and I started homeschooling, we began with her asking me about some of my favorite things. My hobbies, TV shows, songs, etc. and then we based the entire curriculum around these things. One of my favorite lesson topics was *The Price is Right*. I loved that show and my mom is one of the most creative souls I knew. So, for math we created our own plinko board, for finance we created and played the grocery store game, for art we created our own game show logo, and for language arts and writing, I would continue creating my own poems and lyrics inspired by the contestants and their personalities.

I know I am biased, but aside from my mom's creative abilities she was also the best leader. The frustrations with my learning disability and my constant comparing eventually stopped. I was taught to see the good in myself and focus on what I could add to every situation. My lens on life shifted from comparing and measuring myself to others based on what is "normal" to focusing on how I can contribute and what I am great at. She helped me work through every frustration and every emotion with grace, understanding, and love. "Everyone has a role on the team" she said. "What do you want your role to be?" This experience with my mom ultimately encouraged my passion for music, my gift and heart for song writing, and set the foundation for my love and compassion for others. She taught me to see the good in people rather than competing against them.

After only two-and-a-half years of homeschooling, I was testing at the level of my peers (with some additional support of course) and I was able to attend in person classes at school again. Life was good, school was going well, and it was time for my annual Individualized Education Plan (IEP) meeting. The principal of the school, my parents, my IEP specialist, the special education teacher, and my English teacher were all there to discuss an education plan for the future. I felt very supported at the start of the meeting, having all of these professionals present solely to help me. All these people cared about me and my future? I was grateful. Each and every one of them had the purest intentions.

"Brianne, after reviewing your test scores and overall success this year it is time to discuss what your educational future may look like for you." I shook my head with confidence, smiled, and said, "Okay!" Then I heard the following, "If, hopefully when, you get through high school (if you promise to work really hard) your best bet will be attending a community college. This is where you can earn an associate degree. You will probably still be living at home because with your epilepsy it is unlikely you will be able to drive and live independently. But, lucky for you, you have wonderful supportive parents who seem more than happy to help you along the way. Do you have any questions?"

Being a thirteen-year-old sponge, I simply shook my head no, claiming to have understood every word and walked out of that meeting expressing nothing but gratitude to everyone there. Being my twenty-seven-year-old self now though? I have a lot of questions, starting with, "Who the hell are you to limit me like that?!" But we'll get into that more later.

I left the school meeting with my mom who I could see was a little bothered. She could tell I left that meeting more discouraged than empowered. When we got into the car she turned around to the backseat, grabbed my hand, looked me in the eyes, and said:

"BRI, YOU WILL FIND A WAY. DON'T LISTEN TO WHAT THEY SAY. FIND A WAY."

Ultimately, that year, hope was at an all-time high. I had started school again, began to make friends, and was even excited about my extra curriculars. All was going so well and then… I got the news. That hero I just described earlier—that woman who believed in me when it felt like no one else did—my mom? She was diagnosed with cancer. Fuck cancer.

It was a rare liver cancer. I wasn't sure what to think when I was first told the news. I didn't tell many of my friends. Honestly, life went on fairly normally. I think, at the time, my parents were just trying to hide the severity of the whole situation and shield my sister and me. It wasn't until I came down the stairs to our living room to find our priest there that I felt more of an inkling of what was to come. Confused as to why he would be there on a random weeknight I muttered a weak, "Hi Father John." He had a bible in hand and on the table was a gold bowl filled with water. "Mom is receiving the healing of the sick," Dad said. That's when it hit. Maybe this is more serious than I thought.

A mere three weeks passed after that night, when I was sitting in my English class, the principal came to the room and pulled my teacher aside. Next, I hear her say, "Brianne! Come here please." Naturally, I shit my pants. I figured I was in trouble for something. "Yes?" I said (innocently) as I walked over. The class was silent. "Your father's coworker is here to pick you up and take you to the airport. Your mom has been flown to a specialized hospital in Texas for cancer treatment."

We lived in Indiana and I had never been to Texas. Why Texas? I wondered. Why did my mom seem fine but is now in Texas? So many questions. So many emotions. I quickly and quietly grabbed my backpack and coat, looked at my classmates, shrugged my shoulders, and left school with my dad's coworker, Mr. Lawler.

FIND A WAY.

Before I knew it, my sister and I were heading towards the Intensive Care Unit (ICU) of M.D. Anderson Cancer Center in Houston, Texas to be with our mom. I had no idea what was going to happen. Hospitals had been my life leading up to this point, because of my epilepsy. I couldn't stand the smell or that hopeless feeling you get not knowing what is coming next, bad news or good news. I walked along the sanitized hallway and looked at the faces of the strangers I passed. I witnessed every emotion you can imagine all in one place. Some families received the best news of their life, while others the opposite. It was heavy.

When we arrived at the designated waiting area, we were shocked to see so many family members. My aunt, my grandma, my uncle. Seeing the sympathetic looks on my family's faces right before they each gave me a tight supportive hug made me realize how grave the situation was. My thirteen-year-old self knew: Mom was not okay.

The rule in the ICU at the time was that only two visitors could visit a patient at a time. Dad and my sister went in first, then it was my turn. My dad and I walked in together and I'll never forget what I experienced next. So many wires, so many monitors. My eyes scanned the room quickly and saw IV's, breathing tubes, feeding tubes, and the paleness of my mom's face. The smell of a million rubber gloves permeated the room and I felt nauseous.

Mom couldn't speak with all the tubes hooked up to her, but when she saw me, her eyes lit up. I knew she was so happy to see me. I could feel her heart. In that moment I instinctively grabbed her hand. Minutes later, the doctor came into the room. He gave me a warm compassionate smile. I smiled back. I then looked back at my mom's resilient yet exhausted soul. She was fading. Her eyes now closed.

FIND A WAY.

I squeezed my mom's hand even tighter. The doctor walked over and looked at the monitor. He checked her pulse, then looked up toward my dad and stated, "She's taken her last breath."

My mom, the one soul who believed in me, who fought for me, the center of my world, *gone*. The emotion on my dad's face, in that moment, is a sight etched in my brain forever. It looked like he realized he'd lost his best friend mixed with the fear of knowing he now had to raise two teenage girls as a single parent. In there was the pain of having to go on with life alone. Gut-wrenching tears followed. I knew his immediate thoughts were "why me?" and the question, "How will I ever get through this?" All that was on his face. It was beyond anything I could have ever imagined. And I was thirteen.

The following are the lyrics of the song I wrote the night she passed, January 9, 2007.

COLLAPSED

It's like wondering, if the walls collapsed.
In a room you're trapped; in this life there's no map.
Knowing when to go left,
Take your next step, in this life you're left with.

It's hard accepting the truth,
When I can't even feel you.
It's as if I'm blinded and mute.
No sight, no words, no use.

Can this be happening to me?
I'm lost with no company.
In a lifeless, a lifeless room.
With no sense of you.

It's like wondering, if the walls collapsed.
In a room you're trapped; in this life there's no map.

Knowing when to go left,
Take your next step, in this life you're left with.

I'm feeling so alone.
In this world unknown.
But I have a testing chance.
And in life you've got to learn to dance.

Can this be happening to me?
I'm lost with no company.

But you've got to fight,
Whether you're wrong or you're right,
Take that next step, with all your might.

You can do this, it'll be alright.

It's like wondering, if the walls collapsed.
In a room you're trapped; in this life there's no map.
Knowing when to go left,
Take your next step, in this life you're meant with.

"Collapsed" later became the very first song professionally recorded, produced, and released worldwide under Bri Dimit, Storytelling Musician.

FIND A WAY.

Back home in Indiana, I received an outpouring of support from family, friends, and even strangers for the weeks, months, and years that followed. Although I knew I was loved, I felt completely alone.

My dad, sister, and I all grieved differently, and our close-knit family loosened a bit. A few weeks after my mom's death, my dad met Kay, a woman who my sister and I understood was not my mother's replacement but instead a partner for my dad. Experiencing grief and all that comes with it can be scary and I imagine that loneliness I was feeling, he must have felt too. They married about two years later and remain together to this day. As teenagers, my sister and I didn't talk to each other much about our experiences except for the few brief therapy sessions we attended together. I felt my sister focused on her own journey while I sought healing through song writing and asking for support from my immediate community. Still, a void in my life remained and I didn't know how I could keep going.

FIND A WAY.

Six months after one of the hardest experiences of my life, I entered high school. A new environment, a new group of people. High school was tough but experiencing grief in the process magnified it. I always had my music though. Always singing, always writing, and doing YouTube covers in my tie-dyed bedroom as if I was the number one pop artist on the cover of a teen magazine. Music was a light I was drawn to and it always got me through.

I was placed in special education classes because of my epilepsy and learning disability. One of the classes I attended was called "Basic Skills" (as if being in high school wasn't enough of a reason to be bullied). Luckily, I did not experience any seizures throughout my entire high school career. I was even able to get my driver's license due to being seizure-free for five years in a row, something I never thought would happen. I was still taking medication and attending neurology appointments but overall, I felt like I was in a good place and although the majority of my high school experience was challenging, I made some friends along that way that made it all worth it.

Around my junior year the question "what are you going to do next?" was imbedded in (what felt like) almost every conversation. I was reminded of the meeting I had back in eighth grade. What are my options for next steps? I thought. Is college even possible for me? Would I even get in? Could I live independently with my epilepsy? What if I had a seizure?

It was now the summer of my senior year and I ended up receiving three packages in the mail. Acceptance letters to three schools. Two local community colleges and one from a four year "real" college. "Dear Bri, It is with great pleasure to inform you of your acceptance and admission to Ball State University for Fall 2011."

I cried in that moment. Not because I was accepted into a four-year university but because in that moment, I beat the odds. No matter what they said, I found a way. I knew that from here on out, I set the tone for my life. I started to believe nothing could stop me. Not my epilepsy. Not the words and opinions of others. Not all the statistics stacked against me. Nothing. Nothing could stop me. I truly believed that I could create the best path for myself and am responsible for my own success. And ultimately, my mom was right.

YOU WILL FIND A WAY. DON'T LISTEN TO WHAT THEY SAY. FIND A WAY.

In 2015 I graduated with a Bachelor of Science degree from Ball State University while working two full-time jobs, being a full-time student, and living independently, epilepsy and all. The icing on the cake? Ending with a 3.0, the best grade point average (GPA) I ever received in my academic career. I went on to teach early childhood education for a year before I became the youngest (on staff) certified ECE coach for schools in central Indiana in partnership with United Way of Central Indiana. While working full-time as a coach, I had the privilege to apply for a grant and earn my Master's degree. I was accepted to that program and by summer 2018 I graduated with my Master of Arts degree also from Ball State University—with a 4.0 GPA.

Remember that time I sat in a room full of professionals who said "at best" this will be your path? Turns out, actually, you can do anything you set your soul to. You are in control of your life and you are right on track.

If someone tells you "you can't,"
they're showing you their limits, not yours.

DWAYNE-THE ROCK-JOHNSON

As I continue in my professional career, I often refer back to a letter my mom wrote to my sister and I. The first line reads, *"Set out to make a difference, using your gifts."* And so, I do. I made it my mission to amplify the voices of others and started my own full-time business creating opportunities for individuals to feel truly seen and heard, focusing on building a virtual community of hope and healing through music. I have partnered with corporate agencies and not-for-profit organizations, and I speak on platforms around the world, using my gifts to make a difference.

Whether it was my epilepsy, the naysayers in my life, or the statistics that were shown to me, I never let limits defined by others stand in my way. I always said to myself, "Bri, find your way" and instead of allowing my experiences to harden me, I have allowed them to soften me. In doing so, I have gained a deeper understanding of my life, and the lives of others. We all have our own series of experiences and stories. Because of this, I realize it is vital to live with intention, give grace, show up uniquely in the world, and be authentically ourselves. By living with courage, resilience, passion, and soul, **I FOUND MY WAY**.

ERIN MONTGOMERY

Erin Montgomery is a Content Marketing Specialist by day and a 5x published author by night. Erin is a journalism graduate and also holds a certificate in Book Editing. Erin recently published her first children's book, which is aimed to help children of single parents understand that every family is different and that's what makes them unique. Erin is also a single mother to three children who are her everything and lives currently in Ontario, Canada.

WHEN GOODBYE HAPPENS BEFORE YOU ARE READY

ERIN MONTGOMERY

What we have once enjoyed we can never lose;
all that we deeply love becomes a part of us.

HELEN KELLER

It is one memory that I relive on a weekly basis. When I close my eyes at night, I can faintly hear the phone ringing in the distance. I was sixteen, at the height of my carefree teenage years. I was naïve and oblivious to the world around me. Nothing bad had ever happened in my life; my childhood was a dream. I thought I was invincible. At sixteen years old I had yet to experience any type of loss. But in that year, I experienced a loss so devastating that learning to live with it has been the biggest challenge of my life.

Travis was my cousin. My mom and his dad were siblings. We were just a year apart and we grew up side-by-side. He was my first friend, as cousins typically are. We welcomed siblings together and taught them the ropes of our family. We showed them how to always get extra ice cream at Nana's house and we showed them the "sweet drawer," which was filled with more cookies and candies than you could ever want.

Our families were close, and we traveled together. Travis and I experienced Disney World for the first time together. We rode *It's a Small World* more than once and got every character's autograph. We took more photos together than I think I took with my own siblings. We discovered ICQ and MSN Messenger together. He was kind and generous, he was always ready to play any game we came up with. He was one of the most down to earth people I had ever known. Everybody liked him. I looked up to him. His laugh and attitude towards life was infectious. He loved life. And life loved him back.

It was spring, the weather was nice, and summer was just around the corner. I was at dance class the moment the cars hit one another. It was instant. Both himself and his friend died on impact. That accident, on May 1st, 2003, changed our family. Travis had turned eighteen two months before, in March. I remember watching him swing off the rafters in our grandparents' garage just two weeks before. He was talking about this club for teenagers and how we should go together. I remember what he was wearing the last time I saw him. I remember how his hair looked. And then in one simple phone call, the carefree joy that was my life with Travis in it was taken away.

The digital clock on my nightstand was glowing red with 5:30 a.m. displayed across it. My VTech blue cordless phone was laying in the charger, its ringing becoming louder and louder. Why wasn't anyone answering the phone? After a few rings I rolled over and tried to croak out a hello. I remember the words on the other line, "Travis is dead" and they repeated it twice. All I could muster was a whisper of, "what?!?" And that's when the caller realized that I wasn't my mom. "Find your mom," he said.

I remember everything about that run down the hallway. I burst through my parents' bedroom door, cordless phone in hand, desperately trying to get my mom to take over the phone call. She kept telling me to hang up, that it was probably the wrong number. She wasn't listening to me.

So, I said it: "TRAVIS IS DEAD!"

I blurted it out so fast, she didn't seem to believe me. Then she grabbed the phone and quickly put on her clothes as my dad ushered me out of the room. Back in the hallway, my sister poked her head out of her bedroom door, wondering what all the commotion was about. She burst into tears when I told her what I had heard on the other end of the phone.

The rest of that morning is a bit of blur. My sisters and I spent a lot of time sitting on the couch, waiting. What were we waiting for? I am not sure. Maybe we were waiting for my mom to call us and tell us that I had been wrong. That it wasn't really happening. Maybe I was waiting for her to tell me that he didn't die, that he just got hurt in that car accident and he was going to be okay. Or maybe I was simply hoping that it was a different Travis, not my Travis. Not my cousin. Not the person who I went through life with, who I grew up, who I thought would be with me through every adventure life threw at me.

I was not equipped to be the oldest cousin. I was not ready to be the one: the one younger cousins looked up to. The one with all the answers. How was I going to show the younger ones that I was strong, that everything would be okay, when I could barely hold myself together?

His death was the first time in my life where I experienced gut-wrenching grief. I watched a parade of students, from his high school, walk down the main street towards his house and gather on the front lawn with candles and signs. I attended every memorial that was held for him. At his funeral I stood in awe as fifteen hundred people packed themselves into the church. It was amazing to see how many lives he had touched in the short eighteen years that he spent with us. I knew how much he meant to me, but I couldn't believe how much he meant to all those people.

I vividly remember looking out at the crowd from the front of the church, on the day of his funeral, a reading tucked in my hand. I remember swallowing the cries that were begging to escape before I could even begin to start my reading. I was shaking as I held onto the podium. This was it; this was goodbye.

After Travis left us, I missed two weeks of school. When I returned, I was different. I was not able to focus, nothing made sense. I spent most of class doodling RIP notes in the back of my notebook. My friends drew me pictures, gave the best hugs, and were so patient with me. But nothing could bring back my first friend, my cousin, the built-in best friend who was supposed to walk through life with me.

After the car accident, I decided that getting a driver's license wasn't for me. It took me two years to work up the courage to take my test. I was terrified of being in an accident and losing my own life or causing an accident that took away someone else's loved one. My parents didn't allow us to drive in cars with young drivers. We walked to school while our friends drove. Our parents drove us to every hang out session while our friends all piled in the car together. And quite honestly, I don't blame them. At the time, my teenage brain was so mad about how "strict" they were, but now I can see they were also scared.

No one had expected this. He wasn't sick. We weren't prepared to lose him. You never expect to lose someone so young. Parents and grandparents shouldn't have to bury their children and grandchildren. But that is the position we were in. That was the hand we were dealt. I was sad, scared, heartbroken, and unsure of how to move forward for a long time. And there are still days that I experience some of that sadness and heartbreak.

All the experts say you go through five stages of grief: denial, anger, bargaining, depression, and acceptance. But quite frankly I think I skipped the first stage. Denial was never an emotion that stuck with me, except for those minutes that felt like hours, that I waited on the couch after handing my mother the phone, where I hoped she'd come out and say, "wrong Travis." Maybe it's because I was the one who initially answered the phone and I heard the truth in that brief, one-sided conversation. Maybe if I hadn't picked up the phone that morning, I would have dwelled in the feeling of denial a little longer. I remember the anger very well. It stuck around the longest and probably still lingers a little bit. I was angry at the Universe, but I was never outwardly angry. I was angry that he was gone, that I had to bury him, that he had to miss out on the life he loved so much. I was angry that his brother would grow up without him. I was angry that the stress and utter shock and heartbreak of his death had changed our family. There were times where I begged God to let me change places with him or let him have just one more year. But no matter how many times I begged or offered to trade places with him, of course, it never happened and deep down I knew it never would despite how earnestly I begged. But for some reason you always have this little, tiny bit of hope that maybe, just maybe, if you begged enough, God would bring him back. But *he* didn't.

I never sought professional help after his death. It wasn't something that I asked for or something that was ever offered to me. And to be honest, as a sixteen-year-old, I probably would have denied the help anyways.

Roughly four months later, I started to realize that I needed to live again. If not for myself, then for him. I needed to follow my dreams. I needed to be the older cousin, the example, that he was. It was my turn to step up, regardless of how hard it was. It was time for me to live the life that he would never be able to.

It's now been nearly eighteen years since I lost him. While his death was one of the hardest experiences in my life it has also taught me how to move forward, I have learned to live with his loss. Losing Travis made it necessary for me to find my strength, and it has given me a reason to live each day to its fullest. There is never a day that passes that I didn't think of him. I have pictures of him in my home, his teddy bear from his room sits on a shelf, and I talk to him because somewhere inside of me I know he is listening to me. It's funny how death can teach you how to live. But that's exactly what it did. I have been able to move past my gut-wrenching grief and find peace with it. I will forever miss him, but I also know that he would want me to live my life and follow my dreams and do all the things he would be doing if he was here.

Since he has been gone, I have grown up, got married (and divorced), and had children. I have told my children about their Uncle Travis; they know who he was, and how much he would have loved to get to know them. But a piece of me also knows that he does know them. He loved them before he sent them to me. And I know he still watches over them every day. I know because they have told me.

When my kids were super little, between the ages of two and four, I can remember them staring into the corners of the house, or laughing randomly at nothing. I can't say I ever really believed in ghosts, but spirits are different. His spirit is there; it always has been, and it always will be. I can feel it when I am driving, or when I am at a family gathering. And I know my daughter feels him even though he died before she was born.

One day that sticks out in my memory. It was a weekend, nothing special, just a quiet weekend at our house. My daughter was three years old. We were in my bedroom; she was facing the mirror and I sat behind her braiding her hair for the day. She started waving and smiling into the mirror. I laughed. She caught my eye in the mirror and said, "Do you see him?" And I was taken aback.

"See who?" I asked her.

"Him," she said as she pointed into the mirror. "Uncle Devin's brother, you know the one who died."

She was seeing him and engaging with him in that moment, and she wasn't at all scared. She was happy and excited. In that moment

I felt this overwhelming feeling of relief: relief because he was there, because he was watching her, because in that moment I knew he had never really left us.

Since the moment I lost him, I have experienced so many life events without him. I went through driving school, I graduated high school and college, traveled to Australia, got married, had babies, experienced divorce and single motherhood. I often wonder if my life events, the paths I took, if they would have been different if he was here. Maybe he would have steered me in a different direction, maybe his advice would have changed my mind on decisions I made, maybe I would have ended up in a different place if he was here.

I know that I can never know if my life would have had a different course. I know that I can't change the decisions I have made since his death. But one thing I know for absolute certainty is that every decision I ever made in my life I made thinking of him and how he didn't get the opportunity to experience what I was about to do.

Graduating was a bittersweet moment; I was excited to embark on my college years but also sad at the realization that his life was taken from him just two months before he was set to graduate. His death has made me more appreciative of the life events that I did get to experience. I felt all those events more because I felt it was my responsibility to feel them for the both of us. I knew he wouldn't get the opportunity to experience life the way I was but maybe just maybe if I tried hard enough, he would somehow get to live through those events with me. When you lose someone who was important to you, I believe that you carry them with you through everything in the hopes that their spirit gets to see or experience a taste of what they had to miss out on.

Death marks the end of something. The end of a life. But it doesn't close the chapter on that person. Travis' death showed me that while I can't carry him physically with me, I can still carry him around through the triumphs and the failures in my life. I can still have a chat with him when I need advice. I can still visit him. I can still see pieces of him in the people around me. And for that I am forever grateful. Grateful that I had the opportunity to know him, grateful that he was able to teach me the importance of every single day that we are given.

It's important to remember that while losing someone is painful and doesn't always seem fair, it's that loss that teaches us the importance of life, of togetherness, of forgiveness. Losing him was not something I was ever going to be prepared for, but it was something that showed me how to love, how to dream, and most importantly how to hold the people who are important to me closer.

Every day I wish I could have one more chat, one more hug, or one more ice cream cone with him but in some ways I still can. I visit him at his gravesite a few times a year and it is no longer a place I go to cry, it's where I go when something exciting is happening, it's where I go when I need to share a secret, it's the place where I find comfort. Because I know that even though he can't respond he is always listening. And there are those simple signs I do see that show me he is still with me.

We don't get to decide who stays and who goes; if we did everyone would live forever. Saying goodbye and letting someone go is one of the hardest things to have to do but it's also a necessary lesson in life. My cousin's death, while tragic, taught me life lessons I wouldn't have learned otherwise. His death was a steppingstone in my life that I needed to be the person I am today.

Every day I think about him and I glance at his picture on the shelf in my room. Every day I touch the bear that used to live in his bedroom and after nearly eighteen years old I can still smell the faint scent of his cologne. These are the things that give me comfort each day. I know that he was sent here to fulfil a purpose and while his time didn't last nearly long enough it lasted just long enough for him to create a strong family bond between myself, my sisters, and our cousin that we will always hold onto.

He may have only been eighteen, but in his short years he touched more lives than most of us can reach in a lifetime. Death took him too soon, but his life left a lasting impression on the people that knew and loved him. It taught me about resilience, strength, and to always move forward. It made me realize that life is not something I can take for granted. I need to live for now. I need to take every opportunity that comes at me. I need to share my story. I need to show people that there is life after death. That even when death comes and ends the life of a loved one that in some way, they will live on with you.

Travis showed me how he lives on with me. While I won't get the opportunity to see him face to face, I know he is there. He listens, he comforts, he protects, and he cheers me on from heaven each time something incredible happens in my life. I know this and my kids know this and at the end of the day that's all I can really ask. If he can't be here physically at least his spirit is here with me. And every so often when my two-year-old giggles to himself, or stares into space, I know he is interacting with the soul of the man who would have been a pretty incredible influence in my kid's lives. And that brings me comfort. That makes all my heartache seem a little less heavy.

There are no goodbyes for us.
Wherever you are,
you will always be in my heart.

MAHATMA GANDHI

CASSANDRA NAGEL

Cassandra is an entrepreneur and empowerment/life coach who is driven by multiple passions. She helps women globally to break free from their past, their pain, their patterns and their programming. Those who have worked with Cassandra have experienced massive shifts in mental health, relationships and everything in-between. Based on her certifications and education, she uses a multi-disciplinary approach to healing.

Cassandra currently lives in Ontario, Canada with her 2 children and husband.

RISE UP

CASSANDRA NAGEL

Would you believe it if I told you everything that has happened "to you" and everything that you have experienced is formulated perfectly for you? Would you believe that these experiences happened to help you grow your soul?

The art of *Kintsugi or Kintsukuroi* in Japanese culture is the art of repairing a crack in broken pottery with lacquer dusted with gold, silver, or platinum. This highlights the history of the piece rather than disguising it. As an Empowerment and Mindset Strategist, I've learned how to turn what I perceived as broken pieces of myself into the mindset shifts that help me every day.

THE EARLY YEARS

My life didn't start in the same way as many others. In fact it started and ended within the first few minutes after my very first breath. I flatlined shortly after birth and was then revived to continue this adventure we call "life." I didn't really grow up in the simplest of ways, either. Our family struggled financially and there were some dark heavy clouds that loomed over us. I remember my mom often saying, "Our family just doesn't have good luck; we aren't those kinds of people."

In my younger years I grew up primarily with my grandparents as my mom worked several jobs to put food on the table. I never felt like we went without, but I definitely saw the difference between how we lived and the lives of other kids I went to school with. My grandparents even lived for free in an old, abandoned school. I can still see it in my mind's eye today. The teacher's lounge was converted into a mini apartment with a small kitchen-dining room combo. Two steps away there was the bathroom. Three steps the other way and it was the living room and a door to the bedroom big enough for only one bed and a dresser. That was it. They didn't have to pay a cent. The only thing they had to do was clean the remainder of the facility after a wedding or a bingo night or other events were hosted in the gymnasium.

When I was five years old, my stepdad joined our little family. Roughly a year later my little brother graced us with his presence. Unfortunately, my brother was very ill as a baby. This meant that I spent more time at my grandparents' home and I was also able to participate in the summer camp held at the facilities. I was just a little girl without a care in the world. As time started to pass however, I could see the stress overcome Mom and Dad.

My brother was in and out of the hospital. This meant less time working and more stress for our household as money was already tight. My grandmother decided to take on two other children to babysit. I was used to having her all to myself. I began to feel alone as she also had less time for me.

THE TEENAGE YEARS—ABANDONMENT

Belief in oneself and knowing who you are,
I mean, that's the foundation for everything great.

JAY-Z

Our younger years provide the foundation to which the rest of our lives are built on. This foundation shapes who we are and our values. We grow and build from there. I blamed my brother for taking my mom away from me more and I went through a patch where I really was unsure whether my dad wanted anything to do with me. That and all the teenage hormones created a lot of family battles.

When I was twelve, my mom and I had an argument. I told her I was running away and never coming back. Her response was to throw my social insurance application form at me and tell me I needed this to get a job, so I better figure out how to complete it before I go. I realize now that was her way of saying "don't go." When I got up to my room, I turned the paper over, and then saw the application was already filled in. I glanced at it quickly and just before tossing the paper on the floor, I saw that a man's name that I had never heard before had been written in as an answer to "birth father." I looked at this not once, not twice, but probably fifteen times, and for the first time in my life I said aloud: *Who the fuck is Terry?* A sentence that became a staple of mine throughout the years to come.

My head was spinning. I began to question my reality as I knew it. Who was this man? Why was his name there and what had my mom and dad been keeping from me? I questioned it all. I knew Fred, who I called "Dad" wasn't my birth father; I knew he was my stepdad. However, I was under the impression that another man, James, was. Until the age of six, I used to see James regularly and one day he just disappeared, never to be seen again. I do not recall if I even questioned why he never returned until I held that document that day.

Suddenly a deep sinking feeling came over me. This wasn't the first time I felt this feeling of dread. It was the same feelings I had felt many times over. Feelings of insecurity and loss, feeling withdrawn and cut off from the world. I felt like I wasn't good enough and I didn't deserve to be loved. Two things that didn't help the situation are that we had just moved recently and were now a six-hour drive from the rest of our family. And secondly, my grandmother had recently passed away.

I literally had no one else to lean on besides the two people who had been lying to me. I felt completely and utterly alone and abandoned. In that moment of seeing Terry's name on that paper, I recall feeling so torn and broken to know that not only one perceived father figure had left my life but in fact two of them had.

For years to come, I wondered what this man, Terry, looked like and what he may have been going through on his end. I wondered if he thought about me over the years and whether he had other children. I wondered what was his profession and whether I looked like him even in the slightest. I also questioned why I wasn't deserving; why I wasn't good enough for him to come find me?

When I was eighteen, I asked for my mom and dad's assistance and found my birth father. Terry and I met. We had a paternity test done and—boom—from that point on we spent time forming a relationship. It was very weird to share things with a man that I had never known but who also held such a prominent title in my life.

Not everything was smooth. Old wounds opened for my mom. I was the target who received the backlash. After all, I was the piece tying her to Terry, the problem in that equation. I know now she did the best she could in that time. I would hear one story about why he had not been in my life from my mom and an entirely different one from Terry. It was like being in the middle of a tug of war battle where my brain was the unraveling rope. I spent many years building up illusions within myself that people could not be trusted. That I wasn't worth anyone sticking around or fighting for and that I would never amount to anything. I was broken.

YOUNG LADY—I THINK NOT...

Promiscuity is a drug. It starts as a form of therapy but it ends up intoxicating.

REBEKAH SANTERENA

One thing that I failed to mention above was that our family suffered from many addictions. From alcohol to drugs to secrets and promiscuity. You name it and I could tell you who in our family was addicted to it.

In my adolescent years I had fallen deep into the land of promiscuity. It wasn't until later in life that I realized I was in search of the love that I felt I didn't receive as a child. I took it from every avenue and corner I could. I was always eyeing up what my mom would call "the flavor of the week." Every time she uttered those words, I would cringe inside knowing this was not the future I had envisioned for myself.

All I ever wanted to do was make my parents proud. I had visions of talking on a big stage and helping people change their lives. I always felt I could have helped my grandmother too and so many others, had I just had an opportunity to listen and talk with them. But at this time mental health still carried a very dark stigma around it. I decided to jump in and start learning more about the human brain and how it functioned, the conscious vs subconscious, left brain vs right brain and so forth. I would find myself constantly in the self-help section of the bookstore. I was so excited to learn and even decided to apply to study psychology at university. I thought this would help me sort out my family's "brain functions" as well my own.

THINGS AREN'T ALWAYS AS THEY SEEM

I received many acceptances from universities, and I vowed that this was going to be my turning point. I knew in the depths of my heart that there was more to life and we didn't need to live in suffering. My dad regularly worked twelve to sixteen-hour days often seven days a week just so we could get clothes for school, food on the table, and get the bills paid.

I was so excited for a fresh new beginning and a leap in circumstances through getting a degree. My birth father and I had frequent discussions about my future and created a whole new course of action. However, as we know, the Universe always has a way of testing our strength. Plans fell through and my last resort was the only decision I had left. I moved forward taking Business Administration at the college down the road from my mom and dad's instead of what I really wanted.

I took this hard and started to blame myself for everything falling apart. Again, I felt broken. Over the year, I fell short on achieving my own goals which I would abandon to do things for others. I was here again. A disappointment. I moved onto finding love again through external resources. I wanted to regain control, and this was the only way I knew how. I was in constant search for approval and literally filled my days with offerings for others.

My mom became ill and because of that, I dropped out of college; or maybe that was just my excuse. I was so overwhelmed that I simply stopped it all and distanced myself from everyone. I took on three jobs to keep myself busy. Upon reflection, I realized this was not in fact solving any of my issues, rather it was just prolonging the inevitable. I now needed to grow up and take responsibility of my own life. But how?

I decided I needed to break away. I packed up and planned to move in with a friend. We weren't moving that far but it was enough to get me out of my parents' basement and into much-needed responsibility. And life was pretty great. I met Vanessa, who would become my bestie and play a massive role in my life. We met while we both worked at the mall. She was at the flower shop and I at the General Nutrition Centre. We were instant friends from the day we spoke.

My boyfriend at the time also worked at the GNC. We talked a lot about how the future would look. I told him about my dreams of being a speaker on stage and helping others. I told him of my dreams to build a million-dollar company and change the legacy of my family.

He laughed and said, "You? Help others?"

I was instantly defeated yet again. Right... how could I forget I was the broken girl? How could someone make you feel like such a fool with just three words?

A couple of weeks after that, we broke up. I found him at a bar with another girl. Silly that this had to be the reason for a breakup. Heartbroken and confused as to why people could not love me, I set forth with my plan anyhow. I wasn't giving up on myself this time. Instead, Vanessa and I did the inevitable and partied more. I like to think a little wiser but if the streetlamps could speak they may have stories to tell. We have some phenomenal memories. After Vanessa's shifts at a local bar, we would karaoke with my roommate and his friends and we had a blast. This was where I discovered the true healing powers of pickle juice and hangovers. But that's a different story for a different time.

During one of our bar nights Vanessa and I changed things up a little and ended up at a bar that we didn't frequent often. That was the night that I met Jason, the man I am lucky enough to call my husband. I fell so head over heels in love. I thought my life was changed forever and we would live happily ever after—the end. Oh boy... was I mistaken!

MR. RIGHT

My husband and I spent years on what appeared to be growing together in bliss. We had dreams and aspirations of what our family would look like. We both had amazing and thriving careers. We built a house together, got married, and had kids. Being a parent meant so much to both of us as it gave us an opportunity to showcase the growth we had made as adults despite the disappointments of our childhoods.

I always knew Jason would be an outstanding dad. We are both able to be hands on with our own kids in a way that our families never were. Sometimes we laugh and question if this is truly how we pictured it. Our life often consists of cross over hockey runs and sprints from one city to the next. Truly though, our life looks picture perfect... on the outside.

The inside however, was drastically different depending on the day. Our friends saw it at parties when alcohol got the better of us. With everything we had both experienced in our early years of life we had come to believe that neither of us was worthy of love and that no matter what we did we couldn't do it right. This was haunting us. It put a very unusual pressure on both of us and led us to many more arguments, disappointments, lost jobs, and failures while both of us striving to always be right. Being wrong only brought us back to our wounds and made us feel like we were in a million pieces. We were attempting this thing called *life* yet we were both equally lost.

During this time, Mom's health took a downturn; she suffered for years to the point that it all became unbearable to us all. On February 27th, 2018, I received a phone call from Dad: "Cassie, Mom is in the ER. I need you to come. I just can't do it. I need to take a break, I haven't slept."

"No problem, Dad," I said. "Be there soon." I wanted to vomit. I knew my dad had endured so much over the last few years.

As I was driving to the hospital, I had a sinking feeling. I just knew this wasn't going to be good. I had an argument with hospital staff as they did not want to admit my mom. This was followed by three weeks of agony and lots of talking about what was going on. I even yelled at a doctor in a room of patients. Something was seriously wrong with my mom and I wanted answers.

The next morning as I was preparing to go to the hospital, I received a call from *that* doctor, the one I had yelled at. "You are right," she said. "Your mother is dying."

This was the one time in my life that I didn't want to be right. I so badly wanted to be wrong. I would have done anything for a different outcome. The reality I was facing was that my mother had cancer and had been misdiagnosed for years, pushed off as having ailments for which nothing could be done. Over the next few weeks, I spent day and night with my mom whenever I could. We were able to talk about so much in between the moments of lucidity on her end as the medication that was keeping her pain free made her sleep a lot. It was bittersweet as I had yearned for these conversations over my lifetime. Had I not been such an asshole kid, I thought, I could have harnessed this time sooner.

On April 20th, 2018 Mom passed away. I stayed by her bed side for twenty hours the day she passed. I had this weird, gut feeling that I needed to step away. I called my brother and his girlfriend and we went to lunch. That one hour created a guilt that stayed with me for months.

While we were at lunch together, I received another phone call that made me almost vomit: "It's time," the nurse said. Just as we were heading back to the hospital I got stuck at the light. I knew it right there in that moment that my mom's soul left. I started to cry and was so angry. *Why? Why would someone leave me again?* My fear of being abandoned came up firing from within.

Mom was fifty-five years old when she passed; my grandmother was fifty. I knew she didn't want me there to witness her soul liberating itself. It would have been too difficult. I know this because just a few years prior, we were there when her own father passed away. She carried that feeling with her watching her father take his last breath and didn't want us to have that same feeling. She did it for us.

Over the years I had heard my mom say repeatedly, "If I live longer than my mom then I have accomplished something." Or "I am going to die young because that's just what women in our family do, Cassie. You will too." I remember answering her, yelling back, "The fuck I am—I am living until I am at least 92!"

I went over this time and time again. Until one day it hit me. The *self-fulfilling prophecy we speak is powerful.* This is why I became a coach. Helping so many reprogram their minds is a soul-purpose I am dedicated to. As time went on, I fought the grieving process and dove into so many different healing modalities to distract myself. I was fortunate at the time as I worked in a naturopath's office as a registered massage therapist. I dove so deep into healing that I woke one morning while at a business retreat and messaged my husband. I told him that life was too short and we needed to figure out what was going on because I refused to die in my fifties like my mom. If we didn't address this, the stress of our lives would kill me.

THE FALL BEFORE THE RISE

I was ready to face the fact that I had lived a life in which I allowed my mind to dictate every step of the way. I wanted so badly to leave my husband and run away. Not because we didn't have the ability to repair and rectify what we had, but because I wanted to leave him before he too abandoned me. I thought, who would want to be with someone who was so broken and could just die?

My husband and I argued constantly and started resenting each other. In conversation (if you can call it that) we would both go on attack. In brief moments of pause, we also had times of reflection which in turn would return the love and joy we had for each other. One second, we were enemies, the next best friends. It was literally just a mash up of everything we had experienced together in our seventeen years together.

In 2019 we separated for a month and then came back together in December just in time for 2020. We knew inside our souls that we are meant to change the world hand in hand, side by side. It will not always be pretty and will take a lot of work. We have had many conversations and there is always going to be room for growth that is for sure. The beauty here is we made a choice to face this crazy world together and decided to work with each other. We sat down and got real with what we had been telling ourselves for years. We learned through our coaches, studies, and books that wounded people tend to hurt other people. We hired coaches who could call us out on all our bullshit beliefs and hold us accountable. Most importantly we decided to take *massive action* to growing ourselves as individuals, as a couple, and as a family. We sat down and really looked at what a solid foundation of love looked like. We talked about how we could incorporate it into our parenting to help heal generations to come. We decided we would be the legacy changers.

THE RISE

For years I was trying to fit in with the crowds. My fears of abandonment and being broken told me I was different and could not. I felt as though the only way I could achieve and sustain true love was to give up every single inch of who I am to appease others. I now know, that not fitting in means we are meant to stand out, and lead with impact. I remember the stories I heard from my mom way back about that strong little girl I was. I also remembered the broken pottery pieces and realized we are no different. We simply must fill the cracks with gold, silver, and platinum to highlight what has made us who we are today.

Reaching out and seeking out professionals to help me navigate the parts of my life that felt dark and lonely while shifting my mindset has allowed me to lead my family to become the legacy changers we are meant to be. My own work, combined with their guidance, has allowed me to see that life happens *for* me, not *to* me, in a way that has taken me from being that little girl living in the shadows of her fear and poverty, to being not only CEO of my life, but also the CEO of my own business. From generations settling for death at fifty-five, we are set to thrive in life well past our nineties. From scrounging for coins to creating six and seven figure salaries. And from feeling abandoned and broken in life to loving, crafting, and creating healthy relationships with my husband and children.

I will always have moments that I fight myself and my mindset, just the same way each of you reading this will and do. I became an Empowerment and Mindset Strategist to help other women and men around the world turn their obstacles into advantages. It's simple to sit here and gather information then do nothing with it. However, the ability to rise up and make shifts happen comes when you can implement that information into your daily routine. Step by step. Habit by habit. Everything that you have overcome throughout the entirety of your life is simply to help you grow and liberate your soul. I urge you to remember where you came from. That no matter what, no matter where, or how, you have the ability to rise up from anything. You can completely rewrite your story. The main thing that matters is that you stand up and make that decision. Look at your past and admire it for the wisdom it has provided you. This is the foundation to building your revival.

Our destiny is not determined by the number of times we stumble
but by the number of times we rise up,
dust ourselves off, and move forward.

DIETER F. UCHTDORF

*It took me quite a long time
to develop a voice,
and now that I have it,
I am not going to be silent.*

MADELEINE K. ALBRIGHT

FRANCA NAVARRA

Franca Navarra is an International Best-Selling Author, certified Master Life Coach, Motivational Speaker, Yoga Instructor and Reiki Practitioner. She is also the CEO and founder of Universal Coaching International, who has helped thousands of people worldwide to achieve their goals through empowerment seminars, coaching sessions, workshops and social media videos. Franca is a passionate lover of life who enjoys entertaining family and friends, traveling and relaxing with a great book.

I FINALLY CHOSE ME

FRANCA NAVARRA

I have always loved to express my joy for life through movement. Even as a child, when I was as young as three years old, I can remember being carefree and spirited. I would flip, twirl, and dance at every opportunity I had. As I moved freely, I felt absolute bliss— liberation and pure happiness—running through every cell of my body. My childhood through to my early teens was the most joyous time of my life. Everything in my world was sprinkled with fairy dust and sparkles.

It does sound like I lived in this Disney fairy tale, doesn't it? But that is how I saw my world, my life. I was creative, fun, and happy. My own little bubble of blissful ignorance. As I headed into my teenage years, who knew that the bubble would burst and my happiness and joy would end for decades?

THE BUBBLE BURST

At age thirteen, my life as I knew it changed forever. Nothing could have prepared me for what I was about to endure. The day my life changed forever started out as one of the most joyous days of my life. On this particular day I was celebrating my confirmation, a Catholic religious sacrament. Upon receiving my sacrament, my parents had a party for me at our family home and invited all my extended family to come over and celebrate what was supposed to be my special day. The party was going great. Everyone was having fun. I truly valued this time together as we all feasted on delicious food, and shared great laughter with each other.

During dinner, my mom had asked me to go downstairs in our basement to get a bottle of soda for our guests. As I was heading down, my uncle-by-marriage excused himself from the table as well. I did not think anything of it as I adored and trusted him. If anything, I thought he was just heading down to use the washroom. As I continued to make my way downstairs, he by-passed the washroom and proceeded to go down the stairs with me. He followed me into the room at the very back of the basement, where we stored the second refrigerator, the one with the extra soda and food. As he followed me into the room, I never suspected that he had an alternate reason for being downstairs with me.

Within seconds, my uncle pinned me up against the refrigerator door. I vividly recall his hand going up my beautiful pink dress. My voice collapsed, I was not being able to make a sound, as my body fought to escape his intense hold. I never felt so scared, humiliated, or ashamed in all my life. When he was done with me, I immediately ran up two flights of stairs to the washroom. I felt so disgusting, so dirty that I wanted to take a shower and scrub my skin right off my body. I remember looking in the mirror, confused and in shock, questioning myself. Had that actually happened?

What do I do now? I wondered. Sobbing and confused, it was too much for me to take in. So, in that moment I turned in prayer to God and to my loving grandfather who passed away three years before, when I was ten. As I repeated the words, "help me," over and over again I found myself instinctively saying out loud, "forgive him. He is sick otherwise he wouldn't have done this." These were the words that were coming through me. By repeating these words over and over I felt a sense of comfort, just enough comfort to help me get me through the party.

Before I left the washroom, I wiped my tears, washed my face, and headed back to the dining room without the soda. I joined the party as if nothing ever happened. And from that moment on, I kept this as my secret and I remained silent for thirty years. Even though he continued to discreetly touch, poke, fondle, and grab me for the next three years after, by the age of sixteen I was able to reduce contact with him. Thus, I was able to ensure that interactions with him were rare.

Out of sight, out of mind was the idea here. But avoiding him and supressing my feelings only created different problems. As such, I became detached from most people in my life, maintaining only a few of my childhood friendships. Trusting people, especially boys, was extremely difficult. I became rebellious at both home and school which didn't go over well with my parents. I thought everything about my life sucked and that everyone and everything was to blame for my misery. Little did I know that blame brings more pain.

At sixteen I desperately wanted to break free from my strict parents and the family rules; I wanted to experience being a "normal" teenager. I remember hearing other girls on the school bus and in the cafeteria talking about hanging out at the mall, about Friday night parties, and whispering about the cute boys they had crushes on. I listened with envy and wanted to experience this as well. But how was this even possible with my parents' rules and my own lack of trust?

The idea of experiencing my own freedom was becoming more and more compelling to me. I felt like I wanted more out of life but my parents' crazy rigid rules and my fear of trusting anyone kept me stuck in my head. And yet I wanted to experience life like the girls I envied and I also wanted to honor the young teenager inside of me. It took me a couple of years but I came up with the best idea ever: I would get married. That was the answer! Although the thought of being with a boy terrified me to death, marriage became the catalytic force I thought would bring me my freedom.

At the age of eighteen, I set off to college to gain both my education and my M.R.S. I instinctively knew this was where I was going to meet my husband. And of course, I did. I met a very quiet, reserved, small-framed young man who I felt alpha to. Being with him gave me a sense of comfort; I figured that a man with his quiet, calm demeaner could and would never hurt me. He too, was searching to gain freedom from his family and this created the foundation to our relationship. Although we dated for five years before we got married, I never experienced the passionate fairy tale romance love that I read about and watched on the big screen. There was love, we were just not "in love." However, it was because of our commitment through marriage that we created three beautiful biological sons and we adopted a fourth miracle boy together. We were a family.

MY TRUTH REVEALED

It was during the adoption process that I felt compelled to share my history of sexual abuse with my husband. I thought that by sharing the truth, it would free up some of the heavy energy we both had been carrying in our marriage. I also felt that I wanted to put everything on the table, for once to have no secrets, to live more "what you see of me is what you get." For the first time in my life I surrendered to my desire to tell someone. I put all my trust in the Universe and I was ready to receive what was meant to be for our family. But it turned out I had opened a Pandora's Box for myself.

Speaking about my sexual abuse after thirty years, made my abuse real. It was no longer a secret. I realized that I had never really dealt with my emotions regarding it. I never dealt with any emotions about how this made me feel about myself and my subsequent choices to escape my house. By letting out the truth, my pain was now affecting me deeply and seeping into all aspects of my life. The pain creating more complex problems for me especially in my marriage.

This is when I realized I had to find coping skills to deal with my emotions. I decided to join a gym to release my pent-up energy. I did my first class and instantly felt good. The gym became my sanctuary. I loved being at the gym so much so that I became a personal trainer.

As much as the gym was bringing me relief and physical strength, I felt like I needed more. I wanted to find something that was going to give me an inner peace, balance and a calm mind. I took my first yoga class and fell in love. Yoga became my new passion. I was living, breathing, and dreaming yoga. I furthered my practice by taking courses and was soon teaching it full-time. I was feeling great, making my own money, and doing what I was passionate about as a living. I was the most content when I was on my mat; my love for yoga and my clientele shined through me. Often, my clients were compelled to share their personal problems with me and it was an honor for me to help them to the best of my knowledge.

I was asked if I was a life coach so often that I looked into the course and became certified. Although getting all these certifications provided me with a temporary sense of self-worth, I knew deep in my core that the journey to my healing needed to come from a deeper place. Training awakened me to want more of these feel-good emotions that provided me with strategies to cope. I needed to create space within myself, space to allow trust, compassion, and love to grow again. The healing had to come from within me, just like life did; both happen to and from me. I realized that this was my truth. I had an epiphany that through becoming certified and knowledgeable enough to help everyone else around me, I had created a tool box with tools I could use to work on myself.

VICTIM NO MORE

I was in my room crying on the bed after having a huge fight with my husband. This was nothing new; I cried a lot. My husband came into our room and informed me he was taking our youngest to the park. Once they left, I asked myself, with tears streaming from my face, what it was that I really wanted out of life? This was my awakening moment. I answered: to be happy. What a relief to say these words. And yet I knew in order for me to be happy I had to cultivate this process somehow. So, I got out of bed, washed my face, put my lipstick on, because this thing called life was about to get real.

This moment of truth for me meant that I still held love for myself. It was time for me to love myself enough and break free from the emotional prison I kept myself in. All these years I failed to choose what was best for my well-being. Instead, I put everyone else first in my life. I chose to protect my abuser, family, children, marriage, and made that my story. I was done with hiding my feelings. I was done with the façade of being happily married. I was done protecting my uncle for what he did. I was done with the sad ending of my story if I did not change. This was the moment I decided to choose my happiness, my sanity, my life. To finally choose me. I'm changing my story, because I can.

This revelation was the reference point for all the great changes I was about to embark. As scary as this may have been for me, I was ready. It was long overdue. I was open to experiencing joy. I desired to experience the happiness in my own silliness and laugher. This was leverage that kept fear from setting in. I was determined to walk my new path, one step at a time. Sometimes I questioned if I was even on the right path. Of course, all of us question. I would call upon the Universe for guidance and prayed more than ever before. With each step I gained faith.

FORGIVENESS, CHANGES, AND CHOICES

The first area of my life that I worked on was my relationship with my husband. Of course, in the span of our years together there were some great times. However, overall, the marriage was toxic. We knew this and had been going to couples counseling. We decided that after twenty-six years of being together it was finally time to address the truth—we were in a loveless marriage. It was a beautiful realization. Both of us admitted out loud that love was not the driving force that got us to the alter, that, in fact, it was freedom. Also, we shared an internal conflict of having to stay together for the sake of others because of our religious upbringing. We realized that being in the marriage paralyzed us from growing and becoming our best selves. It was a huge relief for both of us when we finally decided to divorce. Since our divorce, we have become friends with each other and most importantly happier and more focused parents to our four sons.

Being a single mom and a free woman, intensified my desire to create and live my best life ever. I realized that to do this, I first had to reach deep and connect, heal, love and accept the inner teenage girl who is still suffering within my soul. It was time to break her free from the chains of her thirty-year sentence, so that I can experience emotional freedom once and for all. For the first time in a long time since my divorce I felt somewhat empowered. And with this feeling of empowerment, I decided that I was ready to seek help. Initially, seeking help wasn't so easy for me because I held some embarrassment to the fact that the coach needs a coach. At first, I figured I could do the healing on my own, but I soon realized that it was too much for me to handle so I put my ego aside. My second choice was to reach out for professional help.

You see, it didn't matter how old I was or what I did professionally, that inner child needed to heal. Healing required me to stop punishing myself and to let go of my ego, guilt, shame and anger.

I was ready to take my power back and my power went beyond my physical being. I always associated being strong and healthy with my body, but through coaching, yoga and my healing journey I realized I am more than my body. I finally made this connection. I am soul and my soul is complete. I am purpose and my purpose was bigger than me. I am power and my power to freedom is determined by me. The third big choice I made was to exercise my power through forgiveness. Forgiving my uncle with all my heart and soul helped release me from the guilt, shame, and anger that I personally carried and owned for something he had done.

MY AWAKENING

My awakening ignited my purpose for living, it deepened my personal relationships with family and friends, and my coaching business went from non-existent to fully operating. Ironically the many clients that reached out to me were from women who had also experienced sexual abuse. The Universe obviously recognized something within me and trusted me enough to help these women heal.

I hold a very special space within my soul for anyone who endured abuse. I authentically understand their pain. Because I am able to empathize so strongly, I'm able to bring a deeper level of compassion, connection and healing to their experience. For many years, I had been looking for my happiness, freedom, joy and peace outside of myself, when in fact everything to achieve all this was within me. I understand today that the power to heal, change, and create the life I want, is within me, in my soul. All my power exists in my accountability, my voice and my decisions. Accountability is important. It is about taking responsibility of what I put out into the Universe. My voice is paramount as I express effectively what it is that I want. My decisions about how I move forward are critical. It has allowed me to forgive the past pains I have endured and given me the gift to practice self-love.

I am not seeking freedom anymore because I know I already have it. I believe that I have the power and freedom to choose and design the life I want to experience. As a result, I choose to create, respond, and live life in the moment and with purpose. Although my life is not without challenges, to me these challenges and how I deal with them are all in creating a strong and positive mindset. These life challenges keep me growing, changing, and evolving. Most importantly, I am constantly learning how to love myself and how to love others.

I FINALLY CHOSE ME

I am delighted to say I no longer use the term, "I was a victim of abuse," but rather, "I am a survivor of abuse." This is what liberation feels like. I finally chose me:

- I finally know the value of my essence.

- I know struggle, defeat and pain.

- I appreciate sincerity, integrity and wisdom.

- I understand perseverance, inner work, and survival.

- I respect myself enough to walk my journey alone if I must, and yet I know enough today, that it is okay to ask for help.

- I show up ready to contribute to the world and I am ok with the world not embracing me yet.

- I am a confident person who is ready to share my life with people who are strong enough to appreciate the woman I have become.

- I truly love the woman I have become… I choose her.

- I choose me.

CARL RICHARDS

Carl Richards has spent more than 25 years behind the microphone, entertaining and influencing audiences worldwide. He is a TEDx Speaker and emcee, published author, host of the Speaking of Speaking Podcast and the founder and CEO of Carl Speaks. Carl helps entrepreneurs find their voice, launch world class podcasts and grow thriving and profitable businesses. He lives with his spouse in Ontario, Canada and enjoys boating in the 1000 Islands.

FREE TO BE ME

CARL RICHARDS

Are you who you claim to be? Is the person that you show to the world, the *real* you? Are you being your authentic self, or do you have a secret identity?

As a child, I loved superheroes: Spiderman, Superman, Batman and Robin, Wonder Woman, you name them. My older brother and I used to play the characters all the time. Our favorites were definitely Batman and Robin. We would make our capes by tucking beach towels into the back of our shirt collars and pretend we were fighting crime, bashing the daylights out of The Joker, The Riddler, or Mr. Freeze. Bam! Zowie! Biff!

Yes, I had quite an admiration and deep interest in superheroes. I watched all the movies, and I knew all the words to the Spiderman cartoon and the Batman TV show theme songs. I even went out as

Robin for Halloween one year and came home with a pretty good haul of candy. As I got older, somewhere around eleven or twelve years of age I could not know that my love for superheroes would lay the foundation for my life. You see, I was developing my own "secret identity." I was scared, confused, and I really didn't know what to do about it. I didn't feel that I could talk about it to anyone. So I kept it to myself.

About the time of my awkward adolescent and teenage years, I found I had very little interest in girls. Sure, they were fun friends to hang out with, but to me, there just wasn't that physical attraction that most of my guy friends were experiencing. Truth is, I was more interested in looking at my guy friends. So… how do you tell your best friend, while he's talking to you about girls, that you've started to see *him* differently? Well, you don't, of course! I definitely had to keep that a secret. I wrestled with this secret identity throughout my teen years and into my thirties.

In the early 1980's, there was a certain type of cancer, a fairly harmless one common in the elderly, called Kaposi's sarcoma (KS). This cancer started appearing as a virulent strain in younger male (mostly homosexual) patients. KS developed in those infected with the human immunodeficiency virus (HIV) which is the virus that causes acquired immunodeficiency syndrome (AIDS). Derogatory terms like "gay disease" or "gay cancer" were being used to describe many of these cases. There were also aggressive forms of pneumonia cropping up in young gay males in greater numbers than before. This turned out to be another symptom of HIV infection. This further contributed to the gay community being ostracized and shunned by the mainstream society.

In the 1980's and early 1990's being gay meant you were different, and not in a good way. Celebrities and famous idols were being forced to disclose their sexuality and their sexuality was put in the spotlight. Icons like Rock Hudson and Freddie Mercury were "outed" and the public curiosity about their secret lives as gay men was linked with life threatening baggage: HIV/AIDS. At the time, there was no cure and no understanding of the disease. Famous people, were being outed and dying and this was happening in families and communities, too. In my family, it was my Uncle Roy. Uncle Roy was not a blood relative uncle but just a good friend of the family who we respected enough to give him that nickname. He died of complications related to HIV in the late 1980's. I didn't know that at the time, nor did I even realize what being gay meant but what my young mind internalized was that Uncle Roy was gay and that his death was linked to being gay. All the reports on the news and other media painted homosexuality with a pretty ugly brush. This was all so new, and it seemed to have come out of nowhere as prior to this, people hid their sexuality and no one talked about it, really. Now, due to the mysterious disease, being gay was dangerous. HIV/AIDS caused panic and shook the heterosexual world as well. Men living their own secret identities that had contracted the "gay disease" unknowingly, infected their female wives and sexual partners. HIV/AIDS also spread through other means as well, scientists quickly discovered, but it was still largely associated with being gay.

With "gay cancer" and "gay disease" spreading across the continents, no one in their right mind would want or choose to be gay! What was the advantage to being gay? What was the thrill and excitement? Even though in Canada, where I live, it was no longer a criminal offence or illegal to be gay, it was still really difficult! If anyone considered you to be gay, you were bullied beyond all recognition at school; called derogatory names like "faggot" and "gaylord."

My family went to church regularly. As a churchgoer, I found out almost every Sunday what God thought of gays. They were evil. They needed to be prayed for. They were bad people. Or, at least, that's the way the message was perceived by many, including me. The minister would stand at the pulpit Sunday mornings and often include gay and sin in same sentence, if not in his sermon, then definitely in prayer. This was not unlike many churches and other religious institutions around the globe as society in general viewed being gay as deviant behavior. Unnatural. A sin in the eyes of God. Oh, and you were a prime candidate for that shameful disease that can kill you!

So back in my teen years, unsurprisingly, gay marriage didn't exist, a gay couple having children was unheard of, and adoption for gay couples was not an option. Sex education curriculum in schools focused on heterosexual relationships only. Not even the slightest hint of gay relationships left the mouths of teachers, some of whom also had a "secret identity." Men who lived together or lived as "boyfriend and boyfriend" kept everything on the QT.

Then there was the fact that my mother's brother, my Uncle Harold was gay. He was very vocal and opinionated about many things. He didn't have a filter; if it was on his mind, he said it, with no apologies. At times he was crass and offensive. To me, he was not a shining, positive example of what it meant to be gay. If being gay meant being like him, I was not at all wanting to identify with it. He was a very supportive guy, just not the kind of "gay" I wanted to be.

Who am I kidding, I didn't want to be gay, period! I certainly didn't choose to be gay. Heck, if I could have sent being gay back, I certainly would have! I wanted to remove the awkwardness that I felt inside of myself with my buddies at school and of course it would have made dating easier. There would be no "coming out," no question about the gender of who I would date and would eventually marry as, of course, it would be someone female. That's what you're supposed to do, isn't it? A lot of people thought if they came out, they would be shunned, lose their connection to family and friends, and in some cases, lose their jobs or credibility. Sneaking around was way easier than actually coming out and facing this likely reality. I had to perfect my double life.

I spent my teen years dating girls and checking out guys. In my twenties, I was getting serious with one girl, while in the shadows having secret trysts with men. Everything was hush-hush. This was long before online dating and smartphone apps, so we would find each other through a telephone personals line and the meetings would be very discreet, usually ending in a trip to a local motel. Like me, a lot of the men I met back then were also deep in the closet. Meeting guys was nothing like it is today. I mean, yes, there were gay bars, but I did not dare go to one back then because what if someone saw me going in or coming out? The default to meeting anyone was those telephone chat lines or the personals ads of the local newspaper. Meeting guys even for short-term satisfaction was, well, work. Which also had to be kept secret.

I dated a girl in college who became a five-year companion. We talked about marriage, kids, all the things young couples discuss. I was kidding myself. I tried to convince myself that my deep-rooted feelings towards men would change. I mean, after all, I had often heard culturally and from church, that being gay was just a phase and it would pass... and in the end, the Lord would forgive me for my sins.

I started my career as a broadcaster in 1997, which meant moving to where the work was. My first stint was in a small remote town some 2900 km (1800 miles) away from home. I stayed with my girlfriend in the first year. We broke up once she realized that she needed and wanted something more immediate in life. Over time, I actually told her I had been dating. She too said she'd been on some dates and was getting serious with someone else. I remember telling her that was great news! She did the same for me. Little did she know that I was dating men.

By this time there were a few, not many, online dating sites. Small towns anywhere are rarely progressive or liberal in any way so it was exceptionally difficult for me to meet guys. I continued to live a dual life, playing it straight with family, friends, and the listening audience. Yet in private and to a select few friends and colleagues, I was Carl, the gay guy. One thing I did that was a step towards being more free was I stopped dating women.

When I would meet people in public they would assume, like so many people still do today, that I am straight. It's amusing now looking back at it. Now when people assume my partner is a woman, I correct them by using his name. Back then though, I had this fear of being judged and viewed as a pariah.

All of this time, I still had not told my family. I wasn't ready. Even though I came from a loving caring environment, coming out as gay just seemed wrong. I had the fear that I would be disowned by my family. I had seen it happen and I wasn't prepared to risk it. In many parts of the world, it still happens to this day.

Globally, being gay means different things. It all depends on where you where you were raised, where you live and what socioeconomic challenges are that go along with it. Gay marriage in Canada for example, didn't become legal until June 2003. In the US, New York State legalized gay marriage in July 2011, eight years after it was legal throughout Canada. In California it is still an uphill battle, even though it has technically been legal since 2013. These are basic human rights that we have come to accept in the western world for the most part. Contrast that to China, where homosexuality has only been legal since 1997. Same sex couples cannot marry or adopt and are not eligible for the same legal protections as heterosexual couples. Factor in the shaming of the family and it is a mess to come out, even if you don't live in China but hail from there. In some parts of the world, like Jamaica, sex between two men is still on the books as illegal and punishable by imprisonment. In places like Dubai and Yemen, homosexuality is also illegal. There the crime carries various punishments depending on region or situation (for example, longer-term gay couples face greater risk) punishable by long prison sentences, flogging, and even death.

Is there any wonder why coming out is complicated? Is there any wonder why people who are gay wrestle with their identity? Depending on where you're from and where you live, being gay can cost you your freedoms, even your life.

I eventually came out to Uncle Harold. To be honest he was not surprised, and very supportive in fact. I remember he said he would always be available if I ever wanted to talk. Still, I kept the secret from everyone else. I had lived with the charade of my secret identity for so long it just seemed normal to keep doing it, but it definitely was my kryptonite. It was draining and exhausting living this way. I would tell my parents how I had made some great strides in my career and met some great people. When the subject of dating came up, I dodged the question saying, "I've had some dates, nothing serious though" and leave it at that.

In the early 2000s, as my career progressed; I had moved to a larger city. There was much talk of gay marriage becoming legal in Canada, though it was met with a lot of backlash. By this time, I was still secret about dating men, but I was also going to gay parties and socials and living as normal a gay life as I could. I actually met someone that I really considered a long-term partner. We casually dated, then ended up living as "roommates" for almost a year. I thought the relationship was going well, but he was not happy and ended it. He was cool living as friends or roommates but wanted to date other people.

I was devastated. Heartbroken. I started drinking more heavily and eating less to cope with the pain of rejection. It was noticeable. I went from a healthy weight of 165 pounds to around 120 in less than six months. My parents kept asking if was ok, commenting on how gaunt I looked. I brushed it off as me trying to cope with the pressures of work, and not being in the best financial shape. I convinced them I was fine.

I was far from fine. I felt I couldn't share with anyone… so I kept it inside. When things like break ups happen, many people share it with their friends, coworkers, or even with their families. There is a built-in support system. Friends, colleagues, and family offer love and support to help with moving on. Yes, I was moving on, but was not sharing. Not sharing was taking its toll on me. I would cry myself to sleep at night and listen to music to make myself feel better. I even tried to immerse myself in community theater, which was a distraction for me, and perhaps a good spot to meet the next "Mr. Right" or at least, "Mr. Right Now."

About six months after the breakup, I visited my family for Thanksgiving. The day before the actual family gathering, I felt that I couldn't keep this "thing" bottled up inside me anymore. On this day in particular, I was sick with fear. I knew I had to tell my parents what was going on even if it meant rejection. I was prepared for the worst. I even packed up my bag just in case I had to leave quickly.

I remember certain details like it was yesterday. I wandered down the stairs to the kitchen where my mom and dad were sitting. They were just about to have tea when I announced I had something to share with them. I sat down and told them, that my roommate was not a roommate but had been my boyfriend for about year and we had broken up. I exhaled, riddled with fear and waiting for my parents to say something.

Instead, silence. The type of silence that was so intense you could cut with a knife. My mom pretty much already knew. Instinctively I think she always knew. After all, it was her brother, my Uncle Harold, who I had confided in years before. Still, she didn't say anything. My dad though, sat there, arms crossed, head tilted slightly down as he processed the news I had just shared with him. My dad had always been as I call it a very "manly man" with his deep resonant voice. He did all sort of things most dads did, or that I thought most dads did: he worked in a factory, muttered really good swear words while doing home renos, and acted like a typical dude. I was on edge, awaiting some sort of response.

"Yes, we've known for a while," my dad said. Then he looked up at me and said the most profound thing: "But you're still my son... and we still love you!" My dad was not usually a man of words, and those simple ones said it all. In that moment a heavy burden was lifted off my shoulders. I had just set free my secret identity and it was OK! I knew in that moment it was OK to be gay! The world still may have not been as accepting in certain areas, but as far as my immediate family was concerned, it was a non-issue. When I came out to my family, I was 32 years old.

Two and a half years later I met a man, the love of my life who would later become my husband. We married in 2009 and still enjoy a great life together. Every day is a new adventure. I have an extended family who loves both of us dearly. We are always doing what most couples do: always looking for ways to make tomorrow even better than today.

Sounds great, right! One slight thing remained. You see, although I had announced the news of my sexuality to my family, friends, and colleagues, I still lived the straight life on the air, and in professional circles. So as much as I was openly gay to my family and those friends around me, I was still deathly afraid to come out on air and be a hundred percent open to all.

I came out on air in 2020. At that time there was much discussion with my supervisor and co-host of how we should handle it. Would it be formally announced? Would it be just something that was nonchalantly mentioned in a normal on-air conversation with my co-host? Would we just refer to my spouse by his name? How would we handle the phone calls we expected? What if there was backlash? What about social media posts? How would we deal with those?

A familiar feeling crept back in, one that I had not felt in ages. The anxiety of impending rejection. It was that same feeling I felt before I came out to my parents. I had that same gut-wrenching and paralyzing fear that kept me leading a double life for years.

There was a reason for wanting to flush out the process. This was a country music station. Though a lot of stereotypes still exist around the music format, most listeners of country music today aren't your stereotypical "redneck." Most are married professional females with families. Yet there was still a need flush out the game plan in case things didn't go as planned.

The day it was announced, there were no phone calls, congratulatory or otherwise. There were no social media posts. There was no backlash. It just started rolling off my tongue like water rolls off a duck's back. Simply and easily, I started using my husband's name and would no longer refer to him as "my spouse." Being able to fully come out and not live a lie or keep a secret felt great! I felt a huge sense of relief. I actually think I gave a big sigh, followed by a little happy dance when it happened. I felt accepted and validated. I had a sense of belonging and that I felt that my life mattered. I no longer had anything to hide and could share openly who I was. Finally, after all these years, I was free to live as my authentic self. That is something that gets lost I think when you're gay.

Still being open in many cases is not easy. Quite often gays live in a place of judgment by others in society. Consider the one of the most unconscious heterosexual couple behaviors, which is the public display of affection (PDA). When a heterosexual couple hold hands, cuddles, kisses or whispers sweet nothings, no one pays attention or if they do, it is viewed as cute. However, in my observations when it comes to a gay couple, people still stare, and give looks if a same sex couple show any PDA. In my experience, there is still a stigma around men publicly displaying any loving affection for one another. For many, it is still viewed as awkward to see and accept.

What had I really been afraid of for all those years? Was it coming out? Was it the rejection that so many gays to this very day are met with when they ditch their secret identities and live in truth? Was it society's reaction? Was it all in my head? Was it perhaps *me* that I was most afraid of?

Whatever the fear, I'm so blessed to be living in my truth. I'm thankful that I have discovered that in life it's better to be honest and up front than to lead others down a path of deception. Most of all, I have learned that it is important to be honest with your own self, follow your heart and live authentically.

As an adult, I have a different perspective on what being a super-hero really means. It is not about the cloak-and-dagger mysterious characters hiding who they are that is part of the intrigue when I was a child. I now realize that it is the mission of superheroes to stand up for what they believe in. It is the triumph of good over evil. It is their job to be fearless and fight for what's right by annihilating injustice, driving darkness out and shining their light. Their thankless acts of bravery rid the world of hate and crime day after day. It's the same for coming out.

Coming out has set me free to be myself, unshackled from the prison of fear and of what other people think. It is about standing in your light and living in your power. It is about courage, being bold, sharing your voice and walking tall without anxiety. Most of all, it is about being your authentic self, mind, body and soul. So far, the greatest evolutions to the gay world, I believe, is that more and more members of the LGBTQ(IA+) world are uniting, standing up, demanding fairness, fighting for justice and equality while showing others that they can do the same.

This has been a long journey to understand who I truly am. After living in the darkness of crushing anxiety and pain of not living my truth for so many years, I am blessed to have the freedom to be myself. No closet, no secret identity, no dual life, no pretending anymore. To be fearless now is a very empowering feeling. My kryptonite of living a double life in the closet is now destroyed. I now have the courage to be myself, and I make no apologies for that. There was a time I didn't have that superpower. I didn't have the wherewithal before to stand up and be ME! Now I do. I am now and forever, free to be me.

When we choose to live authentically
we chip away at other's prisons of pretend
and create an opportunity for them
to walk out of darkness into freedom.

ANTHONY VENN-BROWN

REESHEMAH STIDHUM

Reeshemah Stidhum is a Mississippi native who possesses a Bachelor of Science degree in Biology, and two Masters in Business and Healthcare Administration. She is currently in her 4th year in naturopathic medical school to become a naturopathic doctor. Her interests are on Women's Health, Homeopathy, Dermatology, Diabetes, and Nutrition. Reeshemah currently lives in San Diego, California.

MANIFESTING DESTINY

REESHEMAH STIDHUM

It was a Sunday morning on November 7, 2010. I was driving to Los Angeles from Las Vegas, a four-and-a-half-hour drive. I packed what I could in my car and left the rest in storage. Excited and scared at the same time, I was leaving behind seven years of good, bad, and fun times with friends. I was 32 years old. Due to the 2008 economy crash I was laid off from the laboratory I worked for and driving to LA to live with a stranger who I found through a roommate site.

As I was driving, a childhood friend called me and asked what I was doing. "Moving to LA.," I said. One after one she peppered me with questions based on what she thought was a ludicrous and too-sudden decision: "Are you on your way now? Where are you gonna stay? What are your parents saying about this?" I knew my friend cared for me, but I didn't need to hear her say, "I just think with you not knowing this person, it's dangerous. You don't wanna move back home?" This would be one of many times I would hear people questioning my journey into the unknown. I replied, "No. I made up my mind. I've been unemployed for over a year now. I can't find a job here. Maybe I will find better opportunities in LA." I continued to talk to my friend for a few minutes and we hung up. I was thinking… what if she's right? What if this is a bad idea? I immediately put those thoughts out of my head by pressing play on my iPod and letting music drive the worries out.

The traffic was heavy when I entered LA county that afternoon. I didn't know what to expect of my new roommate. Will I like her? Will she like me? Will she understand my personality? Will we get along? I was starting to voice the same worries I'd been hearing from others. Well, shit I can't turn back now, I reminded myself. I'm here. My GPS indicated I was almost at my destination.

As I pulled up, I called my new roommate to let her know I had arrived. The area looked seedy. "Oh my God, what the hell did I just get myself into?" I said aloud. The apartment complex was old and run-down. I drove to the street to get to the front entrance of the complex. As I parked and got out, I saw my roommate walking towards me, smiling ear to ear. We introduced ourselves and she directed me to the parking space that we would share as roommates. Inside, the apartment was a bit more decent-looking than the outside. We sat down and talked for a couple of hours getting to know each other.

The excitement of moving to LA was short-lived. I checked my visa card for my weekly unemployment benefits and saw there was no money on the card. I called customer service and was told I had exhausted all of my extensions and would receive no more benefits.

I got on the phone and called family which sparked a family intervention with everyone telling me what I should have done, and insisting I come home. Something in me just didn't want to. Maybe it was that voice in my head hauntingly saying, "you failed!" Maybe it was the voice of a class peer from my hometown in Mississippi saying, "Oh, you will be back. They always come back," when I told him I was moving to Las Vegas. Maybe it was me feeling embarrassed at the thought of going back with nothing to show for my time away. Being from a small southern town where everyone knows everyone and their business, I could not bring myself to consider going back into the energy of that town where life was decided for you: graduate from college, get married, and have a family. However, I knew that it was more to life than just graduating from college, working in a local factory, getting married, and having kids. I had to figure this shit out on my own. No one gave me advice when I left Mississippi; now everyone wanted to be Dr. Phil. I felt my anger and frustration levels rising higher and higher.

My goal was always to attend medical school. Because I loved genetics, my plan was to become a genetic counselor, get some experience, then apply to medical school as this would improve my application and make me competitive on paper. I didn't know at the time that California State University Northridge discontinued their genetic counseling program due to low enrollment. But the obstacles didn't end there. There were so many roadblocks that made me re-evaluate and discover myself, my path, and soul purpose.

Applying to jobs brought no luck. My roommate asked, "Do you think it's your name?" "My *name*? No, it can't be." My brother called me and said he reached out to a friend living in LA who was from our hometown. He gave me her number. I called. She told me to email my resume to her. She said, "I know why you're not getting any interviews. It's your name. They aren't used to names like yours out here. They're familiar seeing common names like Amy or Connor. Not names like Reeshemah. You need to change it. Use your middle name, but don't change the resume. Just change your name and reapply to the same jobs using your middle name." Hurt and shocked. I never thought my name was keeping me from getting interviews. I reapplied to the positions using part of my middle name and sent them off by email. I used "Shawn." It was universal and no one would know if I was male or female from the spelling.

The very next day, as "Shawn," I received an email inviting me for an interview at a hospital in Burbank. I had the phone screening interview. After the interview was done, I checked my email. The people from the same organization that interviewed me as Shawn literally seconds ago, wrote to *Reeshemah* saying, "Unfortunately, we decided to go with more qualified candidates for the position." This was my first experience with name discrimination.

I had another interview at the cancer center using my new name. I got off the elevator and saw a male receptionist and told him I had a 10:00 interview. He asked me my name. I said, "Reeshemah. I mean Shawn." He replied, "Which one is it?" I told him my first name is Reesheema and that I'd used my middle name, Shawn, on the application. He checked me in and told me to have a seat.

It was in that moment that I knew I had to kill Shawn as I felt such a disconnect with that name. It made me feel less than because using "Shawn" made me feel like a fraud. "Shawn" wasn't me. Many do change their names and use stage names, but I wasn't auditioning for Hollywood. I couldn't get down with the "fake it 'til you make it" culture.

In June 2012, I started a retail job for which I was overqualified, but I needed it. I went to a two-day orientation later that week. A guy who worked there approached me and asked if I had just been hired. I told him yes. He told me I wasn't going to like it there and I felt uneasy. I always considered myself a "that's a sign" person. My cousin told me not to worry about it and not to give it much attention. But my gut was telling me that this guy was right.

My first day on the job, I was shitting bricks as I didn't have any retail training. Nowadays, the orientation is the training. I was hired to work on the floor, but was put on as the cashier despite my lack of training. After my four-hour shift on the register was completed, I said to myself, "That guy was right: I'm not gonna like this. This isn't me." I walked to my car, got in, drove out of the parking lot, and felt the tears starting. I cried because my gut feeling was coming true. I cried because I felt guilty yet I felt I should instead be grateful. Grateful for getting a job and getting out of a three-year unemployment cycle. After one shift, I dreaded going back to that place. My anxiety got the best of me during my employment there. I was popping anti-diarrhea tablets every day. One day, my coworker, Carol, asked me to ride along with her to an appointment to a spiritual center where her granddaughter worked. Since my arrival in LA, I had been looking for a spiritual home that wasn't religious-oriented, so I jumped at the opportunity.

We arrived at a place called "The Imagine Center," a meditation and healing center. As we entered, I immediately felt a peaceful, calming vibe. We were greeted by Jessica, Carol's granddaughter.

She notified the owner that we were there for Carol's appointment. A few minutes later, a woman in a casual dress came out and greeted us. Her name was Tauheedah. As she walked Carol to the back, I looked around the retail part of the store. Lots and lots of colorful, beautiful healing crystals and tarot decks. This place gave me such a strong, positive vibe that I asked Jessica what other services were offered there. There was one in particular that stood out. It was the Oneness Meditation that was held every Sunday at 11:00 a.m. to 1:00 p.m. I always wanted to learn how to meditate. I read books that included meditation parts at the end of each chapter. But it never told me *how* to meditate, *how* to connect with your inner voice and spiritual guides, and *how* to do proper breathing techniques. I went to the Oneness Meditation and this is when my life changed forever. The energy that everyone brought into the meditation circle felt like a *sacred movement!*

Being part of a sacred circle made me confident in learning how to work with my Divine Team that consisted of my Higher Self, Archangels, Ascended Masters, and Ancestors. I started hating people while working in retail. Many felt entitled and talked to me like I was a piece of shit. Tauheedah told me the reason Spirit placed me in retail was because I wanted to be a doctor. Being a person who wasn't talkative or socially outgoing, Spirit had to give me the tools and skills to be able to speak to diverse people. She told me to diffuse the situation by bringing Spirit in and surrounding and protecting myself with the White Light. It worked. I saw people who would start to approach me, change their mind, and walk past without bothering me. I saw how the negative energy would bypass me like I was invisible, and how a coworker got that belligerent customer. I did this ritual constantly: I asked Spirit to make my shift go by faster and to only bring people of love and light to my lane if I was a cashier that day.

I was living fifteen-minutes from work and renting from a married couple in their late 60's and early 70's, whom I will call Cora and Dan. During my interview for the room, Cora told me she had thirty years of meditation experience and had become so comfortable with meditation that she had out of body experiences. This made me believe that she was someone like me and this was the home for me. However, the warning signs started before I was even six months in. I chose to ignore them as I just didn't want to move again, something I would later regret. This environment came with its own negativity. Cora was very controlling and condescending to Dan. One day, I told her of my plans to apply to medical school. She bluntly said, "You're too old to be a doctor."

I was so surprised that she wasn't open and supportive that I just stared at her. That was not the answer I typically got when telling people of my plans. I recalled many years ago listening to Louise Hay's audiobook *You Can Heal Your Life*. In it she said to never tell people your plans because they would "poo-poo" on them, leaving you with doubts. I never told her anything again. Cora and Dan were always arguing over finances. This environment eventually turned into a home where I hated going to after coming from work. Not just because of their arguments, but I always felt like this environment wasn't truly embracing my quiet demeanor. Their suspicious energy about me made me become so much more reserved. I did not leave my room in the evenings until they went out to eat or retired to bed. After I left work which was sometimes as late as midnight, I would park my car in front of the house and sit in it crying, asking God to get me a better job so I could get my own place. I reached a point where I was happier to be at work than at home.

I thought the opportunity came when I saw openings for a cytogeneticist trainee at a different healthcare center. I had given up applying to trainee programs after being rejected four times before from various hospitals and clinics. However, I took this opening as a sign because it revealed itself after my prayers. I got an interview. On the day of the interview, I didn't have enough money for the gas and instead I used money I planned to use for car insurance money for gas to drive to the interview. I arrived there and my interview went well. Weeks later, I received the email that I dreaded. This was when I really broke down and screamed. I was literally exhausted from rejections. Thank goodness no one was at home. The scream-ing was something I needed to do to release the anger, frustration, resentment, and bitterness that built up inside me over the years. After the release, I called the HR Department to see why I didn't get the position. I learned four positions were available, fourteen people were interviewed, and positions were given to in-house employees. They already knew who they were going to hire. I made sacrifices to drive hours for that interview, which made me even more upset. This was when I finally thought I will never see the inside of a med-ical school. I felt defeated. My childhood dream of being a doctor felt so far away now that I thought I would never reach it.

In June 2016, I woke up and started my day to get ready for work. I went into the bathroom and saw a letter on the counter: it was a thirty-day notice to move out. Cora and Dan had put their house on the market. I was *pissed*! They didn't give me any indication that they wanted to sell their home. And thirty-days? Thirty days wasn't enough time to look for a place where someone would be willing to work with my finances. A place that didn't require you to be full-time employed. Landlords and roommates preferred tenants who would not be home most of the day as being home resulted in higher electricity bills. I wanted a place that would give me kitchen and laundry privileges. These simple things were challenges in LA and I didn't want to battle against them again. I knew all the difficulties I would find looking for a new room based on the years I had lived in LA.

After I received the notice, living there became emotionally charged and unbearable. Cora was bringing me plates of food to my room out of guilt. Almost every day, they came and knocked on my door to ask me if I had found a place yet. I thought this was very suspect and felt like they were rushing me out of the house. I told them I had not. Dan actually said that he's been at home every day and had not seen me leave to look for places. I told him I was looking online and wasn't going to just drive around LA wasting gas if I didn't have any leads. His tone became somewhat aggressive and he asked, "Well, have you thought about getting a second part-time job to help with that?" The audacity of that question! I told him that he had no right to ask me a question like that. Cora, too, thought the question was out of line. I was already angry that they placed me in this position. Dan walked away. I was teary-eyed and told Cora I couldn't discuss it anymore and closed my door.

Cora came to my room one day and told me something that made me lose respect for both of them. She felt so guilty that she confessed what I suspected two weeks prior. She told me the reason they were asking me about finding a place so quickly and why they hounded me every day was that they had a potential buyer. They didn't want the buyer to find out they had a tenant; in fact, she told me they wanted me out sooner than thirty days. They believed if the buyer found out about me, they would pull out of the deal. A buyer would be concerned that I would not move out and they'd be stuck with me after the closing.

I felt betrayed. Despite my financial troubles, my rent had been on time every month and this is the thanks I got from them. Cora repeatedly suggested that I should go "home." Who was she to tell me what to do? I didn't want to go back home. All I could hear was the voice of my school classmate whispering, *Oh, you will be back. They always come back.*

Cora and Dan found a house and began transitioning their things. Meanwhile, I had no place to go. Cora told me that she talked to her brother-in-law who was going to put me in a motel. I was relieved but weary. "Do you really think he will do that?" I asked to which she nodded her head, saying "Yes, he's going to do it." I was unconvinced. "I just know people out here don't mean what they say" but she assured me that he was not like that. "His word is good," she affirmed.

A few days later, I noticed Cora wasn't saying anything to me about the motel arrangements. I had only one day left. I went downstairs to find out what was going on. She told me her brother-in-law had changed his mind and would not be putting me up in a motel. I shouted, "I KNEW IT! Why didn't you say anything to me? Now, I have one more day to find something because when you said he'd help out, I stopped looking!" A few days later, the brother-in-law changed his mind again, this time in my favor. Both him and Dan helped pack my things, loaded my car and theirs too, and we all drove to the Ramada Inn. My paid stay was for seven days. It was not enough time. I had no choice but to move back home. I put my things in storage, left my car at the airport garage, and flew home.

So there I was in August 2016, back in Mississippi. I planned to stay home for two months and then return to LA but the Universe had different plans. I didn't want to see or talk to anyone as my feelings of failure and anger were heavy. My parents couldn't understand why I was so down. I looked into myself and called upon the spiritual tools Tauheedah taught me. I went outside and sat down on the front porch. Once in a deep meditation, I asked Spirit, "What do I do now? I'm a different Reeshemah compared to the girl who left in 2003. Where do I go from here?" I heard the word *healing*. I came out of my meditative state and tried to figure out what the word "healing" could mean in the context of my situation. Two days later, I went into meditation again. I asked that specific question. I was intuitively guided to words: *holistic healing. Doctor.* I opened my eyes and jumped up with enthusiasm. *Naturopathic Doctor*, I yelled! It made perfect sense. Conventional medicine didn't interest me anymore. I immediately got on the internet and searched for naturopathic medical schools. There were only eight at the time. One was in San Diego. This was a sign. It could be the Universe's way of allowing me my desire to return to California.

In January 2017, I applied to Bastyr University California. Before I submitted my application, I asked Archangel Michael to surround my application with White Light to help it lead to an interview. I decided not to do another vision board but to instead use a creative idea from Tauheedah, mentioned in her crystal healing class I took.

Her healing room consisted of statues of the healing team she worked with, including a Black woman statue that represented her. I used this same idea. I bought statues of the Archangels and Ascended Masters who were part of my Divine Team. I was looking for a Black woman doctor statue to represent me, making it feel more tangible. I found one on Amazon that had the white coat and stethoscope around her neck. I bought a small table and placed the statues on them. Every day, I would see this altar, do a prayer and ritual to manifest my childhood dream of being a doctor.

In March, I received an email invitation for an interview. I was excited. I flew to San Diego the following month. Afterwards, I was nervous because I felt I had messed up the interview, but when I considered everything, I knew that I'd surprised myself with how well I'd responded to questions during the interview. I admitted to myself that my answers were actually impressive. I asked the Universe to give me signs to let me know that I secured a place in the entering class. I began seeing and hearing San Diego mentioned on TV. Weeks later, the phone rang: "Congratulations," the person on the other end of the line said, "you have been accepted to the entering class of 2017!" I finally received the "yes" I was searching for, and it opened the door fully. Not to a hospital, lab, or retail store, but to a naturopathic medical school!

I look back on my journey and see how rejection became so draining, both mentally and emotionally. It caused me to feel discouraged and lose confidence in myself. It also caused me to doubt my skills and capabilities. I couldn't see the blessing of returning home because I was so angry and embarrassed about my failures. My fear of failure was so profound that I never gave up regardless of my circumstances. My vision was so strong that I became fearless, and I realized that my actual fear was of returning home and not accomplishing my goals. Spirit took me out of the chaotic energy of LA and brought me back home to readjust, readapt, and refocus. Being home gave me the clarity to see who I am, and where I was going. My childhood home represents a sanctuary for me now; it keeps me grounded. It is a place I took for granted. I saw how I had to come full circle. I left Mississippi as a naïve girl and the many obstacles to success helped me to evolve into a woman of wisdom, a woman of truth, and a fierce, fearless Goddess with a bad ass Divine Team. Words couldn't express how I felt with news of being accepted to naturopathic medical school. I was so grateful to enter into this new part of my journey, my dream. For those past and present that never believed in me, rest assured, that no longer matters. I believe in myself.

Many believe success is about making and having a lot of money. My adversities made me realize it is not. For me, it was never about money. It was about me being happy and living my purpose. The Universe rewards you for your efforts, not the other way around. Material things can be taken away from you in a split of a second. I saw how being out of alignment with my purpose brought many obstacles and rejection. When you are in alignment with your purpose, your path becomes clearer, and doors open for you effortlessly. Life becomes harder when we go against our purpose and do things not meant for us.

My lessons taught me that fear made me hold onto things that didn't serve me or my purpose for far too long. Fear triggered me to self-sabotage opportunities because of past disappointments. I stayed in a place where it was familiar even though miserable because I was scared of what others would think. I wouldn't have known what I am capable of, had I not pushed through my fears and kept moving forward. I became so fearless in my pursuit of my goal that it made me a force to be reckon with. It empowered me to believe I could conquer anything that was truly meant for me.

Rejection is the Universe's way to block what isn't meant for us. It helps provide clarity to reroute and pivot in a different direction. Through these lessons, I realized that rejection is not actually failure. Failure is about making mistakes and learning who you truly are. It's about getting knocked down, crying it out, getting up, and trying again tomorrow. Never giving up. The Universe has enough abundance to reward everyone. I am a champion who rose from the ashes of defeat and soared again to my destiny. I now realize that the rejections were fueling my strength and tenacity. Within the rejections was the key to my victory. When things didn't work out the way I planned and wanted them to, it actually forced me to question what I really wanted. Did I really want to become a doctor? What is happiness to me? To me, being happy with myself, doing what I passionately love and being of service is what true happiness is all about. The defeat made it impossible to see that I had it all along. This is what I believe defines true success.

The blueprint to your destiny is already within you. The key to your dreams is already given to you. You have to believe in yourself with sufficient conviction to unlock the door to your destiny.

There are only two lives we might live: our dream or our destiny.
Sometimes they are one in the same, and sometimes they're not.
Often our dreams are just a path to our destinies.

GLENNON DOYLE

Owning our story
can be hard
but not nearly as difficult
as spending our lives
running from it.

BRENÉ BROWN

MARSHA MYLES TERRY

Marsha Terry is a coach, speaker, author, and Registered Nurse with a passion for mindset transformation. She specializes in empowering men and women to reclaim their voice and walk in purpose. She's the creator of Masterful Mornings—a powerful framework for designing the ultimate morning routine. She has a Master of Science in Nursing with a focus in Leadership and Management and is co-author of *Remarkable Business: Spotlights on Top Professionals and Business Owners.*

THE BIRD CAGE

MARSHA MYLES TERRY

The caged bird sings with a fearful trill
of things unknown but longed for still
and his tune is heard on a distant hill
for the caged bird sings of freedom.

MAYA ANGELOU

THE GOOD 'OL DAYS

Up until I was eight years old, life was filled with fun, friends, and culture. As the youngest of three children, my brother, sister, and I were very close and always played together even though they were much older than me. We lived in the bustling multicultural city, Toronto, Canada. As the city was growing exponentially, many cultures celebrated and embraced their heritage. They established themselves in different pockets as they immigrated from other parts of the world while co-existing with one another in a wonderfully cosmopolitan manner. Although we lived in a very diverse neighborhood, our Jamaican Canadian community was close knit, celebrating traditional holidays through food and music. I would play with my older siblings and neighborhood friends like we didn't have a care in the world. In the fall, my brother would rake the maple tree leaves into huge piles in our yard and all of us would jump in. It was fun and exhilarating! The winters were fairly mild, and we loved playing outside for hours. We went sledding down the nearby hills at the park, built snowmen, and made snow angels. Those were some of the best days of my childhood. I felt like my life was my own.

On any given weekend for no reason at all, my parents would have a basement party. We would hide in the shadows, giggle, and watch the adults dance and be high-spirited until the party was over. The music was always bumping! There were always a lot of people who seemed to come and go. There was never any disorder or disruption, just people living life without limitations. I remember one time after the party was over and all my parents' friends had left the house, my cousins and I snuck downstairs in the early morning. We saw a bunch of beer bottles laying around and half eaten plates of food. I don't know whose idea it was, but the next thing I knew we were trying to get a little taste of the beer from the bottles. *Yuck!* It tasted nasty! We never quite understood the fascination with alcohol.

Even though we had a lot of fun and enriching experiences, my parents were typical Jamaicans and very strict. Although they had both left Jamaica as young adults, they held onto a lot of traditional values. Kids were not to speak unless spoken to. My father always sat at the head of our kitchen table. My mother served him first and would sit on his right side. I would sit beside my mom, while my brother and sister would sit opposite of us. My mom always cooked well-balanced meals. We never ate sandwiches or simple food, only very traditional Jamaican food. My parents instilled in us work ethic, the importance of an education, and being financially responsible. Our lifestyle wasn't extravagant, but we had a good happy home.

ONE DECISION

For reasons unknown to me at the time, my dad applied and got a job at the Tar Sand plant in northern Alberta. Before I knew it, we were packing up all our things in a U-Haul truck and driving across the country. By the mid-summer of 1978, my family moved from Ontario, the biggest province in Canada, to northern Alberta in western Canada, 2,358 miles (3795 kilometers) away. Unlike many other parts of the world, Canadians don't tend to move around the country as much, most likely due to geographical distance from one city to another, weather and business opportunities. We moved from a thriving, exciting city of business, multiculturalism, music, entertainment, adventure, and family to a town nestled in the forest. Yes, from skyscrapers to a one-industry, small town literally in the middle of nowhere.

One decision changed me and my life forever. The carefree summers of being surrounded by family vanished. I missed the different seasons like the changing of the leaves in the fall. The mild winters with our Christmas tree decorated with silver tinsel, gold garland and popcorn on a string would become a distant past. I left my friends, my cousins, and the only life I knew behind. It was definitely a culture shock as this was not a diverse or multicultural community at all. There were very few people in this town that looked like us, and there was no one my age at school with the same Jamaican Canadian heritage.

My family was adjusting to our new environment until an undercurrent slowly started to change things. I can't pinpoint exactly when, but somewhere along the way, my parents started to argue. Our home which once had been fairly calm and even keel was losing that positive vibe. There were days the tension was so high nobody spoke. The energy was disconcerting and uncomfortable. My siblings knew what was going on. Being the youngest, they shielded and protected me from the developing drama in my parents' relationship. Despite the constant discontent, my mom cooked every day and served my dad's food. Some days he would eat it, other days his chair sat empty while we ate. It was hard to imagine this was happening to our family. It was a very difficult time for my mom. Her family and friends were in Toronto and the likelihood of moving back there was non-existent. She could not afford it. There was nothing to go back to. I'm sure she felt trapped and isolated but never said it.

My mother decided at some point to take correspondence courses, similar to online learning today. The difference was a student would order courses through the mail and the material would be delivered to the student in binders. When you completed a unit, you would mail it back to the school for grading and they would send you the next lesson. In the evenings after all the dishes were cleared from the table, my mother pulled the Smith Corona typewriter onto the table and typed into the night, diligently working on her studies. I learned the value of obtaining an education watching her. She may not have realized but watching her taught me to be independent. A seed was planted in me to not have to depend on another person for my well-being and to always hustle and be in a position to take care of myself. These were tough lessons for me to learn at this age. But I watched, learned, and stayed quiet.

OUR NEW NORMAL

The major decision my father made to move across the country led to a chain reaction that changed our lives forever. My mother was missing the feeling of community and connection. So, it was during this time that she found and took us to our new church. Church had always been a central part of our lives, at least to my mom and us kids. Up until this point we had been going to a Baptist church. We went every Sunday. My dad hardly ever went with us. Maybe during Christmas or Easter but going to church was definitely not a part of my father's ritual. My mom made sure we wore our Sunday best every week. If for some reason we didn't go to Sunday School, we would have to sit in the church pews quietly and not move. It was tortuous for us. The most we could do was flip the pages of the hymnals. If anyone one of us moved too much or made the slightest noise, my mom's eyes would penetrate us with a look that set everyone straight.

We left the Baptist church and moved to a new church that had a much smaller congregation than we had been used to. The singing was loud with tambourines and drums. People would dance and sing in the aisles all the time. The preaching was exuberant, and the services were long. The more we became involved in this new church, the more my parents argued and grew apart. This time it was my mom who made the decision. The Pentecostal church was going to be our new denomination.

Shortly after joining, our lives changed drastically. We went from going to church on Sunday morning to going twice on Sunday's, several times during the week and most of the weekends. Church was our life. The basement parties stopped. I wasn't allowed to go to any school dances, parties, nor was I allowed to watch TV. My mom got rid of all of my pants, shorts, and bathing suits. My mom stopped wearing makeup and jewelry. We no longer dressed up for Halloween or celebrated the holidays we used to, including Christmas. It was such an extreme change from the way our lives used to be. It definitely took some time to get used to things. However, since I was so shy and reserved, I never explained to my friends at school what happened. It was confusing to me and I was embarrassed. I went to school with the same group of people all those years. So, they knew the pre-Pentecostal version of me. I'm sure they were just as confused as I was.

Once we were fully immersed in our new church culture, my parents separated and then subsequently divorced. They had been married for nineteen years. Our church family supported my mom in ways that I will forever be grateful for. My mom, sister and I downsized to a two-bedroom apartment at the same time my brother left for college. Looking back now, I understand why my mother found solace and refuge in our church. We had no other immediate family close by. Our church was a supportive environment and we formed new family friends from those who also attended. I saw my mother struggle as she tried to balance our household as a single parent. She would wake up early in the morning and get ready for work. In the winter if the car was working, she'd have to go outside and heat it up before leaving the house. The snow would be so high, or the wind would be blowing fiercely as she cleaned the driveway. The winters in northern Alberta were treacherous, long and cold.

Like many of my classmates, I was a "latchkey kid." I always had my house key on a yellow piece of yarn tied around my neck to lock and unlock the door before and after school. My mother worked long hours in the local department store cafeteria and wasn't always home after school. Despite going to school for administration work, my mom quickly realized that she couldn't sit behind a desk all day. She pivoted and studied to become a certified journeyman cook. Cooking has been and continues to be her passion. Aside from her day job, she took an evening job cleaning. Some evenings we would drive at least thirty minutes from our home to clean an entire office building. There was no way my sister and I were allowed to stay at home alone. Also, we had to help her so she could get the job done quicker. Everything my mom did she did with pride and excellence. She taught us to do the same. By the time she was doing this job, I was a teenager. When we weren't cleaning the office suites during the evening, she cleaned houses on the weekend. I knew money was difficult for my mom, so I never asked for things. I just accepted what I was given and appreciated everything.

By the time my sister went to college, my mom had a better paying job and bought a new house. I went to school, church, and home. That was my life. With my brother and sister out of the house, I felt isolated and alone. I didn't have many friends at church and didn't feel I belonged. I definitely didn't have any other girls who shared a Caribbean background to hang out with. Even though my friends at school were kind to me, I still felt odd. I never felt like I fit in. I looked different and I couldn't do the things they did. If I was invited to birthday parties or sleepovers, I couldn't go. If they went to see a movie or to a school dance, that wouldn't have been tolerated.

Somehow, in middle school I found the courage to join the girls' volleyball team. That was a big deal. I desperately wanted to feel a sense of belonging. I didn't tell anyone at my church. There's no way I could have! The only person who knew was my mother and she never told anyone. I went to every game and played with all my heart. Sadly, we were the worst team in the division and lost every game we played. Silently, I blamed myself. I was the reason we lost because I went against our church rules. I felt like God was punishing our team. As much as I loved sports, I never tried out for any other team sport again in school. I wasn't going to stand between the team and its success because of my religion.

MY DECISIONS

By the time I was seventeen, I knew I was going to leave our little town to go to college. I had decided that I wanted to become a Registered Nurse. I chose this profession in part because I thought I would like it, but also because I knew I could wear a dress or skirt as my uniform. All of the decisions I made were within the construct of what our church allowed. Going to church wasn't just an experience it was a lifestyle. It's outlandish now to think how everything I did was dictated by other people. Every dream I had, aspiration I sought or decision I made was based on the limitations that my environment set upon me. Practicing law wasn't an option because what if I had to lie for a client? Being a doctor would have been too demanding and would have taken me out of church for too many days.

In my young mind it was best to choose a profession that attracted the least attention less resistance by the church. So, whether or not I wanted to choose something else, having the ability to exercise choice didn't seem plausible. As a result of this, I experienced shame, fear, doubt, and low self-worth. I never believed that I was good enough to do anything or had a voice to assert myself. I carried these emotions and thought processes into my adulthood. If I wanted more, I didn't see it around me. I didn't know any female entrepreneurs, doctors, lawyers, or other professionals. Abundance and wealth were not emphasized. I didn't see it in men or in women. Free thinking and curiosity were not encouraged. I was living my life in white, gray, and black and didn't see anyone around me embracing life in all of its beautiful and bold colors. I was trapped and didn't recognize it. I believe that unconsciously, I felt like a caged bird who longed for freedom to spread my wings and fly.

Caged birds grow the most colourful wings.

LAURA CHOUETTE

Throughout my early twenties I continued to live my life according to the beat of a drum that wasn't my own. I was working and going through the motions of life. However, when I was twenty-seven, I made a decision that unknowingly changed the trajectory of my life. I left the comforts and predictability of my life in Canada and moved to Texas, USA. It was the first time, I lived in another country and with no immediate family within driving distance. I packed up all my possessions in thirteen cardboard boxes and two suitcases and boarded a plane heading south, over 2500 miles (4023km) away. If my family had moved across Canada, then I was sure I could make this journey and survive. There wasn't going to be anyone peering over my shoulder, no one watching and reporting what I was or wasn't doing. It was just going to be me and God.

With the guise of my new-found freedom upon leaving the coop, I started dating, dancing, drinking alcohol, and coloring outside the lines! I started to have fun, a little too much fun, I must add. I thought that since I changed my behavior that I would feel like I belonged, that I fit in. Despite all of this, there was still something that was still misaligned. I was acting the part, looking the part, but inside of me was still the caged bird.

MY NEW NORMAL

Within months of settling into my new life, I found a congregation aligned with my core beliefs incorporating holidays, celebrations, free will and my personal relationship with God. My faith in God is and continues to be an integral part of my life. Within four short years of being in Texas, I soared and settled into the next phase of my life and got married. There is truth to the scientific principle "Opposites Attract", because my husband and I were very different. My husband was a budding entrepreneur, outgoing, sociable and very confident. There wasn't anything he couldn't do. He didn't see limitations on his life, only opportunities.

Throughout the beginning of our relationship, my quietness and lack of active involvement about what was going on around us prevailed. I still hadn't learned how to use my voice. My husband made business and personal decisions without much input from me. It wasn't that he didn't ask for my input, I just hadn't recognized I could have an opinion and voice. Leading up to the birth of our second child was when I started to wake up. I decided that I wasn't going to go back to work. I wanted to stay home and take care of our children. We had a lot of heavy discussions about this and in the end, I won. Looking back, it was one of the first times I knew my voice carried weight. When my second son turned three years old, I made another significant decision to enroll in school to advance my nursing career.

Much like my mother, I found an online program and pursued my Master's degree in Nursing. My focus was on Leadership and Management. I began to discover parts of me that I didn't even know existed. I absorbed all the information I could about leadership and transformational nurse leaders. I was drawn to concepts of visioning and creativity, being agents of change, empowerment and mentoring. Although I was familiar with some of these concepts from previous exposure to the network marketing industry, these ideas started to take on a new meaning. I connected what I was learning in my classes and began to discover my inner voice. The feelings that I had of not fitting in, being misaligned started to roll back. A passage in one of my nursing textbooks defined exactly what I was experiencing:

There are three kinds of people: those who make things happen, those who watch things happen; those who wonder what happened.

GROSSMAN & VALIGA PG. 141
THE NEW LEADERSHIP CHALLENGE
CREATING THE FUTURE OF NURSING 3RD EDITION

By the time I turned forty, I decided I wasn't going to watch things happen any longer. I was going to spread my wings and fly. Over the next ten years, I started to lean into discovering my purpose and passions. I discovered that the quiet, shy, introverted girl that

I was, actually had a voice and an opinion. I wanted to share my experience with others. I wanted to empower and inspire other women who felt like they had been trapped and voiceless as I had been for so many years. I began to recognize that believing I couldn't do things was something that others had imposed on me. I gained confidence knowing that I could believe in myself and achieve. I wanted people to know there was hope on the other side of fear. I started to invest in my own personal self-development by attending seminars and workshops. I started to push my fear of public speaking by doing just that, speaking publicly. I looked for platforms and forums to share what mattered to me. I started to engage in difficult conversations with my husband about the things that I wanted and stopped asking for permission. I started to take risks and learn from my own mistakes. I was determined to walk to the beat of my own drum. I was going to release the caged bird from her confinement and let her ascend.

Throughout these transformative ten years, there has been a lot of soul searching, many shifts and accomplishments. Most specifically, I dialed into my gift of listening, that led to sharing and motivating others. Upon finishing my Master's degree, I started working with my husband as the administrator of our physical therapy clinic managing two locations. Having never been in a position of leadership of this type, I learned everything I could about our industry and how to operate our business in a practical way. When I felt that managing the clinics had been running smoothly and efficiently, my soul kept nudging me toward a different direction. This new avenue would be something just for me. I knew instinctively that I should obtain certifications as a life and health coach. I came alive with all the knowledge I gained about personal development. This was my jam, my soul purpose.

Finally, everything that I had been through in my life started to come together. From not knowing to knowing. From being asleep to being awakened. From being told I can't to achieving all I could. I have come a long way from the shy, demure girl who shrunk away from challenges to one who now walks with confidence and grace through her fears. From stagnation to soaring. I am committed to showing people how they can fly like a bird with the most colorful wings. I show others that living life is moving beyond seeing only gray, white and black to embracing their vibrant beauty within themselves and the world around them. Upon completion of my certifications a number of years ago, my wingspan kept growing and reaching new heights. I launched my own life coaching business, joined several women's networking groups and served on their boards and began teaching and speaking at live events to groups ranging from ten to three hundred.

As community and inclusion have always been very important to me, in 2019, I co-founded a non-profit organization called Village in the Valley where we elevate and unite the Black community while connecting cultures in the Rio Grande Valley, located in Texas. I have been interviewed by local radio hosts and several national podcasters relating to my business and my non-profit organization. Through this organization I've continued to serve and inspire our members. I've focused on ensuring my personal passions and professional pursuits remain in alignment.

I have embraced my life and live with purposeful and soulful passion. This is honestly just the beginning and I couldn't be more excited to see the elevation of my path. I am on a continuous journey of transformation and know it is my purpose to help others do the same. It is indeed a lifelong process of growth and change. My heightened level of awareness comes from my practice of meditation, reading, journaling and coaching. I have implemented a daily practice to take time out to invest in myself before I invest in others. I fuel my own energy before I spend it on others. This may sound like I am being selfish, but the truth is, I have actually learned self-compassion. My approach to living is no longer defined by the constructs of other people. I am constantly re-evaluating and discovering what is important to me. My unwavering faith in God and what *he* sees possible for me are deepened with resolve daily.

The relationship with my husband is stronger because we have an intentional relationship. Even my children recognize that I am no longer stressed out, overwhelmed, and just surviving day to day. Children see and learn from their parents, as I learned my core values from my mother. I want both of my children to see and learn from me as the woman that I am today and the one I will be tomorrow.

Since I've come into this place of feeling and knowing, I am aligned with who I am and who I am supposed to be. I now live with bold color from altitudes I never before believed I could have achieved. I have come a long way and am incredibly proud that the picture I am creating is one that I look at each day in admiration.

You have escaped your cage,
your wings are stretched out, now fly.

RUMI

Scars are beautiful
when we see them
as glorious reminders that
we courageously survived.

LYSA TERKEURST

MARIEKE VAN ASTEN

Marieke van Asten is a published author and founder of a non-profit Breadfruit House Dominica Foundation in the small country of Dominica which has been fighting abuse and poverty. A Netherlands native, she realized she was born for a greater purpose and moved to Dominica. Marieke uses her love of art and creativity to help young children be empowered and heal from their traumas.

ART AND SOUL

MARIEKE VAN ASTEN

To practice any art,
no matter how well or badly,
is a way to make your soul grow.
So do it.

KURT VONNEGUT

You would think that getting married to a great guy, owning our own house with a white picket fence, a car, and a dog, plus both of us having a job would be amazing at age twenty-three. I thought so too. Well, that is to say, I convinced myself for a while that it was my dream.

In the beginning, it was a very "Jane and John in the suburbs life," living in the same small town in the Netherlands that I grew up in. About three years into the marriage, the first cracks began to show. That triggered my determination to make my marriage work, and I did everything I could to keep the "perfect couple" image. I vividly recall one day we had a big argument about sex, and I started banging my head on the wall to beg him not to leave me. In the back of my mind, I knew our marriage had died already; I just wasn't prepared to bury it yet. I am not even sure if it ever was alive, to be honest. Nevertheless, I kept taking all the blame and saying sorry for everything. It was exhausting and felt like dragging a dead horse.

We both worked for the same bank, although at different branches. One day HR called and told me that earlier that morning, the branch where my husband worked had been violently robbed, with automatic rifles. He was head cashier at the time and was pushed to the floor with a gun pointed to his head. Fortunately, no one was hurt, that is to say, physically hurt. The robbery changed my husband forever. He went from being very outgoing and fun to be around, to withdrawn and almost anti-social.

In those days, bank robbery was quite frequent, but the bank did not offer any counseling to its employees. Our marriage, already in trouble, kept rolling downhill from there. We struggled a lot, and during those times we did not speak to each other for days. Eventually I found out he was cheating. I think he was too cowardly to tell me that he found love with someone else. His crush wrote him a Valentine's card, and he deliberately left it in the car. When I took the car to buy groceries, I found it casually placed on the passenger seat. It hit me hard and I felt totally lost, like the earth was about to swallow me whole. I don't recall how I managed to get home with groceries, but I did. I threw everything on the kitchen counter and left. It was mid February and icy cold. I walked for hours, completely dazed, and not even knowing where I had been when I finally returned home. I felt hurt, betrayed, and most of all, a failure.

We went back and forth for about a year, I continued to take him back every time he asked for forgiveness. I finally reached my point of no return and told him to move out while I was away on vacation. I sobbed the night I returned home, cried myself to sleep in that empty house. It felt like my all-time low, but I knew deep down it was for the best.

Trust me, I had my share of pity parties and ugly cries. Eventually the time came that I was done feeling sorry for myself; I wanted to get out of the mess I was in. I found myself getting out my paints, easel, and brushes again. Art was my me-time and it really helped me, together with counseling. I was able to see that what happened was a lesson, not a failure. I could admit to myself that I had been so focused on what others perceived as "the norm" that I completely overlooked what I wanted. I realized that life is all about learning.

MORE LIFE LESSONS

I was able to keep my home after the divorce and continued working at the same bank branch, giving me a sense of normalcy. With counseling and the return of my passion for painting, I started feeling happy, going out more, and socializing with friends. I even set up an art studio in one of the spare bedrooms.

This one particular day didn't start off being different than any other, but the Universe certainly had other plans for me. I was at the train station, as usual, heading home from work when I noticed this well-dressed, good looking man that I hadn't seen before. I didn't approach him, and I was sure he hadn't seen me anyway, or so I thought. Months went by without seeing him again, until that one day… there he was again. This time, he introduced himself. Bento was very charming, he complimented me and seemed like a true gentleman. His stop on the train was before mine, and we started waiting for each other every day after work to travel together. In those short trips, he shared bits of his struggle with a difficult divorce.

Eventually, I invited him over, and we talked for hours over dinner and drinks. He was very forthcoming and good at portraying a dark picture of how his life was at that moment. On many levels, I felt his story did not add up. Yet, I chose to ignore that and enjoy his attention and company.

I am not sure if I have ever really been "in love," but I felt I was falling for him. In hindsight I was in love with the idea of being in love, not the man himself. As a child, no one told me that I was loved. Not that they did not love me, it just was never said. As a result, I strove to be the nice little girl, to make sure people would love me. At the same time, as complex as we are, I also had a sense that I was unworthy of love. This feeling had become part of me and actually prevented me from accepting that I was indeed deserving of love. Consequently, I would hang on to the first man who showed interest in me. I would let his charm overwhelm me and cloud my judgment of whether this was a suitable life partner. My inability to love myself made me feel I was unlovable in general. And because I do not believe in coincidence, the Universe presented me with opportunities to change this belief about myself. Granted, this relationship certainly turned out to be one huge learning in many ways.

After his divorce, Bento moved one hour drive from where I lived, and we spent many weekends at his new place. And although the lack of furniture and sleeping on a mattress on the floor did not bother me, I could never sleep. It was a major red flag, but like other warning signs, it was one that I only acknowledged years later. Over time, he started to become jealous, and although I did not like it, nor was I used to it, I put up with it, allowing it to develop into a bigger and bigger problem. The tricky part was that he was very charming when he wanted to be. I also stopped my creative me-time and became completely absorbed in making sure he would not leave me.

An undeniable red flag was when the first time he hit me because he thought I was seeing someone else. We were in the bathroom, and he confronted me. He never waited for my answer and just hit me on the side of my face. I fell on the edge of the bathtub and for weeks I was deaf in one ear. I went to see my doctor, where I made up a story because I felt too ashamed to tell the truth. Fortunately, the damage was not permanent. Bento went out of his way to apologize and even told me to hit him as well, which I did not do.

We moved on from that incident, and things were good for quite a while. After about three years, we decided to move in together. There always were some unexplainable incidents, more little red flags in disguise, but I chose not to listen to my gut feelings. I had taken it upon myself to prove to *him* that I was reliable, trustworthy, and lovable. I felt I would be able to fix his twisted vision of me and the world around us.

He landed a great job as a civil engineer and earned twice my salary. The two salaries combined allowed us to afford a lovely and spacious house so that when his two children visited, each had their own room. Everything seemed to be coming together. We were so happy as we toasted the new century in our home on December 31st, 1999. Little did I know what I entered into.

I sold my house, boxed everything up, and in early January, we were all set up in our new home. He brought nothing except his computer, clothes, and a bunch of books. I was happy to share; after all, I was in love with him. That's what I chose to tell myself at the time anyway, and you might see a pattern here. I was blissfully unaware of the dark clouds approaching.

My life collapsed slowly, almost without me noticing it, almost. Over time I stopped visiting friends because his constant phone calls would end my joy before it even began. The only visits I did not compromise were to my parents. I went to see them every weekend and Bento almost never came with me, yet he would call several times to make sure where I was. He would call me first on my cell phone, then on my parents' landline, disguised as a courtesy call. And at the same time, he would ask me when I would be leaving so he could track the time I took to get home. I reluctantly addressed his jealousy, and that sparked a rage I had only witnessed once before—the time he hit me with such force I ended up deaf for weeks.

In the midst of all this, Bento had his first epileptic seizure. I had witnessed seizures before in public because the village I grew up in is home to an epileptic research center. Yet, when it happens to the person sleeping next to you, it is different; it was horrifying, and I was not sure what to do. Sadly, this was the start of many, and his seizures were always sizeable and prolonged. The diagnosis meant he was no longer allowed to drive, and that made him more and more dependent on me and forced me to give up more of my time and space. In those days I started to feel very isolated, but I couldn't admit to myself, let alone others, what was really going on.

ART BECAME MY REFUGE

Bento consequently had a heart attack and later on a lung embolism. In the madness of all that, I tried to keep up appearances for my family and friends. I was not sure what was wrong with Bento mentally; he became increasingly unpredictable. He subsequently lost his job and, through a bizarre turn of events, he also lost the right to any unemployment benefits which put a heavy strain on our financial situation. Even though I worked forty-hour weeks, my salary was still only half of what his once was. He would lock himself in his room and smoke weed all day to self-medicate. It came to a point where I told my parents to keep my savings to prevent it from literally going up in smoke. As he was not allowed to drive, I had to drive him to get his weed every day. I tried saying no, but that did not go down well so it was easier to just say yes. I felt trapped in a situation I didn't know how to handle. Between working full-time, trying to deal with all financial stress, and keeping a 'happy' face I was exhausted. Bento's behavior became more erratic; he was living in his own delusional world, and demanding sex four times a day, every day. I say sex but it felt more like rape since no was not an option. To endure all this, I somehow taught myself how to mentally remove myself from the situation. That was the only way for me to survive this ordeal.

Without noticing it, I had lost myself. I stopped going out because the moment I left, Bento started calling me and, not answering his calls meant repercussions later. In my mind, I felt like the only safe space was the one square meter around me and, even that got invaded. To survive, I negotiated, one evening a week to paint, without interruption. In the smallest bedroom, I would listen to music and paint. Most of the time I silently cried my eyes out, not knowing what to do or where to go. Often the entire page or canvas came out black. Painting felt good and became my outlet for all the emotions and feelings that I could not discuss with anyone. I felt lonely and alone amid all this chaos and, painting became my safe haven, my beacon of hope for those few hours every week.

A turning point came when Bento assaulted a neighbor in the middle of the night for saying hello to me in the supermarket. To this day, I am grateful that our neighbor called the police. Bento was admitted to a psychiatric ward. That same morning I went to see my doctor and found out, for the first time, that Bento had been a diagnosed schizophrenic for many years. Both his children were at our home that weekend when all this took place, and his daughter told me that when she was five, he did the same things to their mother. With tears in her eyes she told me that she remembered it vividly. That stuck in my mind and I still recall her trauma and hopelessness. His daughter has to live with this memory for the rest of her life. Children do remember early childhood trauma which became one reason I set up a non-profit years later.

If all that was not enough, the bank informed us they would foreclose on our house. I had chosen to buy food and utilities instead of paying our mortgage. I never felt more ashamed and courageous than the moment I called the bank's debtors' department. I had only one month to sell the house myself. And low and behold, the house got sold within two weeks for the asking price. I was even granted five months to find myself a new place to live. Bento was still in the psychiatric ward during that time. The sale of the house felt like a miracle, like the Universe was helping me to get back on my feet.

I felt the Universe wanted to make sure I learned from my experiences and stood behind my choice to end the relationship to save myself. I found a safe apartment in a good neighborhood. The bank approved my mortgage after a special committee assessed it. My many years working in banking came to good use navigating this.

My soon-to-be ex was released from the psychiatric ward while I was away on a well-earned vacation in the United States. I felt compassion for him—he was severely mentally ill, had no house, and no job—so I had left him a key to my apartment. We had an agreement that he would move out before I came back; of course, he was still there when I returned. I had an unforgettable relaxed holiday far away from everything and I had enjoyed a lot of "me" time. The day I came home, my "how unhinged is he at the moment" antenna switched back on as soon as I opened the front door and saw signs he had not moved out. I knew things were bad when I found clothespins in very odd places, like a cutlery drawer, and between my underwear.

The minute Bento entered the front door late that evening, I felt his rage. He started rambling about my vacation, convinced I had been sleeping with every Tom, Dick, and Harry in the USA. He threatened me by tapping his finger on my collarbone, something he frequently did before he went in the hospital. I always felt extremely intimidated by that, all the while he was cursing and screaming at me.

At that moment, I had reached my limit and felt a sense of calm coming over me. I knew this was when I had to choose me. I called the police, and the dispatcher was really helpful and told me whatever happens, to stay on the phone. Not long after that, the police arrived. I stayed in the kitchen out of sight while Bento kept rambling about what a bad person I was, how I slept around, tried to poison him, on and on for what felt like the entire night. I cried, I sobbed, and I prayed, begging God to make it stop. Together with a crisis nurse and psychiatrist, it took them four hours to persuade him to leave voluntarily. I packed some of his clothes, and the police escorted him out in the early morning of my 45th birthday—what a way to start a new chapter in my life. *A new chapter indeed.*

At the same time that I purchased the apartment, I had also changed jobs. I was changing my life for the better. It felt like the wheels started to turn in my favor and I was so encouraged by all of it. My doctor set up therapy with a psychologist. Eventually, I started making plans again. I had many things I wanted to do and discover. First on the list was volunteering abroad. To challenge myself, I chose a Spanish speaking country and started classes as I did not speak the language. My teacher was from Venezuela, and with her advice, I decided to go to Costa Rica. It proved to be an excellent choice, and it impacted my life in so many positive ways.

Traveling alone threw me into the deep end and made me come out of my shell. I had to overcome my fear of speaking Spanish since hardly anyone spoke English. My local host family was amazing and welcomed me into their lives with open arms. They even took me on a pilgrimage site trip.

The host was a lay minister in the Catholic church, she invited me to join her for Sunday church service. I felt very humbled by how devoted people were. And service was a lot less tedious, even though I only understood maybe ten percent of what was said. In the church on the pilgrimage site, I saw people going down on their knees, holding up their newborn babies and shuffling to the altar on their knees while they prayed. I admired them for their enormous faith. I was invited to spend a day at a local high school talking English with the students. I did a presentation for adult students at the University of Costa Rica and a guided tour in a botanical garden and many more memorable trips and places I would have never visited without this incredible family.

I volunteered in a small primary school in a poor community and the school reflected that. There were only four classrooms and a kitchen. You had to bring your own toilet paper and there were no lights in the washrooms. On an overcast day, it was a challenge to find your way around. It was sobering to think this was their reality every single day, mine only for those few weeks. Everyone was very welcoming, and I soon became part of the school. The children taught me so much more than I could have ever taught them.

With all the donations I collected from family and friends I was able to buy a lot of arts and crafts materials to do fun projects with the children. Together, we even painted the school in bright colors. My creative heart was filled with joy and I slowly realized what creativity can do. Without words you can express how and what you feel.

My host family had a little front porch; the tiniest one you can imagine. Every evening I sat outside in my favorite rocking chair and watched the world go by. Their dog, Perla, would often come and nestle herself on my lap. As I gently rocked back and forth, I felt happier than I had felt in a very long time. I felt free from all the negativity in my life and my outlook was brighter than ever before. I often recall that place in my mind as ultimate happiness.

The beautiful adventure in Costa Rica planted the seed for leaving the Netherlands to work with children and creativity. How, where, and when, I had no clue, I just felt that huge desire in my heart and soul. And the Universe heard me and gave me what I asked for in an unexpected way. Not long after I returned to the Netherlands, I met Leo from Dominica on an online dating site. I wasn't interested, but he kept contacting me. I didn't even know where Dominica was. Originally, I thought it was the Dominican Republic which is Spanish speaking. Well, Dominica is not even close to DR. Dominica, is a small English speaking Caribbean island which is part of the British Commonwealth, located in between Guadeloupe and Martinique.

Leo spoke with great passion about his farm. I decided I wanted to visit him to meet in person. Another big adventure that not everyone approved of, yet I felt compelled to go. When I got off the plane, the warm smell of the tropical rainforest felt like coming home. We immediately clicked and spoke for hours while he was smoking meat in an old oil drum. And so, my long-distance relationship started. We each traveled back and forth many times. After six years though, I wanted to move forward and create a life together. I pictured myself living on the farm and working with the village children. To my surprise bringing up moving to Dominica wasn't met with the enthusiasm I expected. Even though this was a red flag, something indescribable pulled me to Dominica. Even my boss told me, Marieke, you seem happy in Dominica, have you considered moving there? Like it was written in the sky, that's how many signs pointed in that direction. So, I went ahead with my plans.

I worked up the courage to tell my parents, and my dad said to me, if it makes you happy, go. Never in my life did I feel more loved than when he said that. So, after months of preparations, I sold my house, quit my job, and went on a plane to Dominica.

Before landing, I felt like I ate a brick; my gut told me my life was about to change. I could have never foreseen how much change it would bring. When I arrived, Leo acted strange and unwelcoming. Close to three weeks after I landed, I ended the relationship. Later on, I found out that he had been seeing other women all the time we were having our long-distance relationship and wanted me out of his house. It was two weeks before Christmas, and it was my loneliest holiday season ever. I rented an Airbnb, a rundown house on top of a hill, with only rats, birds, and termites as house mates.

Trapped on that mountain, because of the bad weather, I did a lot of soul searching whether to stay or go back to the Netherlands. In the end, I decided to give life in Dominica a chance since I loved the island and her people so much. I hardly knew anybody, and volunteer work seemed like an excellent way to meet new people. Early in January, I started working as a volunteer both at a pre-school and a charity. Another new chapter started, part of it working with children and the other part involved using my creativity.

PASSION AND PURPOSE

2017 was a turbulent year. Not only did I step out of my comfort zone to start my new life, both my parents died as well, twelve weeks apart. While I was attending my mom's funeral in the Netherlands, a category five hurricane destroyed the island, my beautiful Dominica in mid-September.

I was unable to return right away due to the conditions in Dominica. Compelled to do something, I decided to raise funds to help to rebuild the country in the hurricane's aftermath. It was December 11th, before I was finally able to go back home. Home…

that's how I felt. The devastation was beyond belief, and the many international aid organizations created multiple opportunities for me. I got to know many people and learned so much while working with them. It felt so good to be able to contribute. The incredible work UNICEF did with their Child Friendly Spaces really caught my attention. They helped children to deal with emotions through creativity. I became more and more aware of my mission in life and why the Universe brought me to this beautiful tiny Caribbean island.

Fast forward four years, I started a foundation, a non-profit, for children in Dominica, named after my favorite food on the island, the Breadfruit House Dominica Foundation. Dominica is a poor country and children have a lot to deal with: trauma from the hurricane, poverty, abuse, neglect, and domestic violence are all too common.

From my own experience, art and creativity have always given me an outlet to express myself, helped me find strength and served as my light in an otherwise dark world. With the foundation, I want to spread that same light to all the children in our program. The mission is to gift these children with purpose, give them hope, a voice, make them be seen for who they are and allow them to dream. I want them to feel they are worthy of love, give them an outlet to express themselves by inspiring them to tell their stories through art and creativity. I get to brighten the children's day with glitter, glue, paper, and scissors, but I am also a beacon of light for them to shine and grow to become empowered adults.

Following my heart and finding my purpose has brought me so much joy and fulfilment. I am happier now than I have ever been in my life. I now know that once I found my purpose, my life changed completely. The Universe put the right people in my path and resources appeared unexpectedly. Showing up as and for yourself is healing, and that shows on the outside as well as the inside. That does not mean it is always easy, but it is so worth it.

Art is a wound turned into light.

GEORGES BRAQUE

KAREM ZAFRA-VERA

Karem Zafra-Vera is a published Author, Mediator and a Transformation Coach. She is a certified Conflict Resolution Specialist in the State of Florida specializing in Family and Circuit Court. Karem has been studying personal development for over 10 years. After being trained by PGI, she transitioned to becoming a Mind, Wealth and Transformation coach, now founder of Next Level Consulting "Mindful With Karem." Karem is a mother of three young adults and married to her high school sweetheart for 24 years.

IGNITE YOUR PURPOSE

KAREM ZAFRA-VERA

The wisdom of others
can ignite your passion,
uplift your spirit and motivate you
to reach your full potential.

MELISSA ESHLEMAN

Who am I? I have asked myself that question quite a few times. I always end up with all the titles we are so used to using to identify ourselves: I'm the oldest daughter of three, first granddaughter to both sides of the family, the eldest sister, wife, mother, and I'm an entrepreneur. And yet I am not fulfilled. So, I asked myself, *why*?

I come from a beautiful, closely bonded family. We are part of a large extended family, but we consider our family to be just the five of us. This is probably because my parents moved around a lot and they had to depend on themselves to make things happen. Thankfully, my childhood memories are more on the happy side than not. I feel so blessed for the childhood that my parents gave me. Not to say there were no hard times and that all my experiences were good. Although, I had the belief and expectation that as the first born, I needed to strive to be the best, so I was an overachiever. Funny how we begin to screw up our kids based on these types of assumptions. Yet, we say to ourselves that with our own kids, things will be different.

I also feel that guilt is a major trait in Latin culture; it's part of our DNA. I felt guilty if I did something for myself; it is a trait I find is common in Hispanic women. I do not mean that I felt like I didn't value myself at all. I just was not aware of what it meant to value yourself at the level I now understand.

Looking back, I can now see some of the beliefs I held that were not empowering. As mentioned earlier, being the oldest of three came with a massive amount of weight and responsibility, but it also came with some perks. I like to say that I was loved and am loved in a way that makes others wonder why and what is special about her? I have always felt like a bright shining star is always lighting my path. I've grown up with a feeling of uniqueness. I traveled a lot and never stayed in one place too long. My mother more than my father loved traveling and we moved around quite frequently. By the time I was seven years old, I had already lived in Colombia (where I was born), Venezuela, Puerto Rico, and St. Louis, Mo. My circle of friends has always been minimal. My family has always been my center.

As the oldest I felt a great sense of responsibility. I'm not sure why I took on that belief. Most of the decisions I made day to day were made thinking of what was right for others. What was the right thing to do? Am I hurting someone's feelings by not doing what they want me to do? Am I disappointing someone? Let me take care of everyone's issues and try to bring peace or happiness to everyone.

Or was is it this need to control situations? Why? Why was control so important? What was I unconsciously protecting myself from?

Even as a young girl, I tried to make everyone happy or at least to protect their feelings. It was not only with the immediate family. I also cared in this way for other people. My guilty conscious was the hardest obstacle I've had to overcome in my life. If I said no to anything, I would feel horrible. I would spend so much time and energy thinking about how things would be better if only I, that person, or this person did this or that. I would go the extra mile to make someone feel better because that person was not showing up per their expectations so I felt I could help them. I would find myself speaking to and for everyone, always trying to bring more unity or peace and understanding.

After several years in the family business, I went back to school, graduated, and became a mediator. As a professional, I continued in the same role. I did not see that my job was exactly what I have been doing my entire life. Except this time, through my work, I was empowering others to resolve their problems and be happy or whatever that meant for them.

THE BEGINNING OF THE TURNING POINT

Have you ever felt a blow to your heart that shifted, moved the ground you walk in? I think that was the beginning of my turning point. My brother and I have always been very, very close. I have always felt that we have had our backs in everything, kept our secrets, and had a profound bond that I know not everyone gets to have with their siblings. My brother was and still is the child, the sibling that usually gets everything he wants because he has been the baby of the family and the only boy. His laughter and his funny personality when visible are addicting and you just want to give him anything he wants or do anything he wants because you love him so much. I remember working one day and we got into a massive fight for reasons that are not important to my point. However, it was the turning point for me to stop hovering, worrying, or living my life on the side lines while making sure everyone else is okay. When I say living on the sidelines, I mean making day to day decisions based on how it would impact someone else instead of my kids, husband, and *me*.

I realized at that moment that I needed to live for me and for the life I want to give my children and have with my husband. I had to stop putting them in third place as I was doing. I felt a release that day and with it, I did feel emptiness and detached. I felt selfish without the guilt I usually carried. My shift was so pronounced that my mother, days later, asked me what was wrong and why I was so different and cold.

Change doesn't always come smooth. To be honest, I felt like a cold bitch! Now, why is it that I felt the need to call and identify myself as a *cold bitch*, and not just as a woman who was starting to recognize her inner truth? Wow, this self-judgment is the very reason most of us hold ourselves back and do not risk peeling the layers and growing. We dare not flourish or see who we really are under the layers of society, expectations, influences, and beliefs. Just because I decide to step into my truth doesn't make me a bitch, selfish, or stuck-up. It only means I have stepped into a new level of awareness that is seeking to be expressed and seen. My true *"I Am."*

A change of circumstance happens as a result
of a change in your state of consciousness.

NEVILLE GODDARD

CANCER HIT HOME

I grew up with my mother being sick all the time. I have experienced my mother on her death bed twice. I have seen my father at points that felt like there was no return, times when he thought he would lose her. The ambulance was called to our home so many times and I have visited too many hospitals. As an adult, it was almost expected and no surprise when we heard anything from a doctor, or when my dad called to inform us that she needed to be hospitalized. Too often my brother and I had to make the decision for my father about whether to have our mother hospitalized. I knew what that felt like. But when my dad was diagnosed with cancer, it was an entirely new ball game. This was a man that had never been hospitalized, who would go on fruit diets, who took no medication and believed you could remove a headache with your own mindset, simply by holding your temple (which is true, I have come to learn). My dad was the one that liked to go for walks and have a more active life. He read anything and especially loved to read about the human body. How could it be true that he was the ill one?

Life had just flipped on me and it made no sense. Cancer hits everyone else, not my family, I thought. In our family history, cancer was prevalent, but never did I imagine it would hit my father. It changed the direction of my life. They say things happen for a reason and everything is meant to be. That there are no accidents. We may see them as accidents because it's not expected. But I did not fathom how much my life would change. Cancer peeled away layers of me that I was not aware needed to be peeled.

THE JOURNEY

I started to question life. What do I do? Why am I doing it? What do I want? Am I happy or just going with the flow? Do I know how it *feels* to live fully? What have I accomplished? I began to see how I was limiting my life in so many ways and not even noticing. I was settled into habits that silently snuck in. It's this invisible enemy that shows up as part of our lives. Wow, I did not know that I had stopped desiring things because it was so easy and normal to shut down the dream, and my desires. I realized that I was living life because it was what we are supposed to do. We create these habits and if we do not notice that in doing so, we create a comfort zone that does not serve us. And it is not till something shakes us, like in my life my father's cancer, that you do wake up!

I woke up, but it wasn't immediate. It wasn't like one day I said, "Wow I'm awake." It was more like I saw a little more each day. I began to question and think on a deeper level than just what I had to do to get through and live another day. Is that not crazy?! Living as if life was not a gift. As if we don't have this amazing power within ourselves. I can't begin to tell you the massive amount of life force within ourselves that we only see when we just begin to live with more intention.

I started to ask myself where did I lose sight of the gift of life, or my dreams? I know for me the settling was due to finances. It was those unempowering conversations we have with ourselves when we want something and we say *next time*, or *this obligation is more important than my desire*. That idea that we *need* to be responsible, and that responsibility means we have to figure the other priorities out before we take care of what we *want*. Once I started coaching others,

I realized that I, myself, was so not used to dreaming. I had been telling myself I was *fine*. *"Fine"* a horrible word to adopt. That's what I did: meshed my dreams to fit my circumstances: It's okay if I don't travel, if we don't go on vacation, if we can't get this for the kids, if I don't shop for clothes. The *if… if… if* started to disappear and no longer showed up. Or if it did, I would shut it down and just go with the flow. What kind of life was that? Seriously, I had no idea that I was living that way. You can imagine that when I began to think deeper, see things differently, and questions things it shook the house of comfort I did not realize I had created. This version of you begins to grow and then life—a circumstance, a significant birthday, an illness, a tragedy—suddenly shakes your ground like never before. That was what my father's illness did to my life. It woke me up.

It was well into my coaching career when I started implementing strategies into my own life. Raising my awareness allowed me to see things with a different perspective; I started using my imagination and dreaming, setting significant goals. At first, when I found myself unable to imagine anything further than my current circumstances, I asked myself why this was so hard for me? I realized that shutting down my imagination beyond my current circumstances had become my habit, a habit I did not even know I had. A habit that doesn't serve me in anyway. This aha moment is like in that algebra class when you cannot seem to figure out how to simplify the formula enough to get the correct answer. And then suddenly you solved a problem, and you are like *OMG… aha …* I see it now. I had plenty of those epiphanies. I changed as I kept asking myself questions, "So where in your life, are you not showing up for you?"

SURRENDERING

Now, let me take you back to that moment in 2019 when I was faced with circumstances my mother was experiencing due to depression. This is where I experienced what surrendering meant. It's not like what you expect. Not surrendering to a friend, a loved one, or a physical human being. This is me surrendering to God, the Father.

Have you ever had a moment in your life that you can honestly feel and say, "Okay! I release control. I'm literally passing the baton and I will follow your direction?" That was me! It was a moment in my life that I felt so directed. I felt a sense of peace, a sense of massive trust in my heart. And I was also experiencing a feeling of desperation I had never felt before.

This is that moment you just sit and cry for a miracle to happen. I knew, I didn't have answers or ideas. I did not have anything in my mind, any expert's knowledge that I could turn to for help or guidance. And it was at that moment that my relationship with God reminded me I was not alone. I don't know about you, but I had this belief of praying like most of us do. We pray with the intention that *he* will helps us but never really surrender to the idea, to the point where you do nothing because *he* will provide. I had not really thought about it before. What did it mean to pray before this experience? Did I even imagine a result? Did I envision anything or just asked for what I wanted and not dive any deeper? Had I previously believed that for what I'm asking would really be delivered? Did I even know what it looked like? Or had the prayer felt good enough that I never felt the necessity to dig deeper and even allow myself to go beyond that of what provided my initial peace. Was my praying habitual, since I have been praying from when I was a young girl? Did I have an expectancy? Could there be more?

The thing that became crystal clear to me was the need to release. Release my control over the outcome, release my expectations, release my judgment, release my fear, release my predictions or the idea to have every answer. Release the sense of responsibility. It was a moment where I felt stripped from everything to gain everything. I did not know this at the time. The only thing I was clear at that moment was I had to turn it to God. To let go and trust that with anything else that happened, I would be guided, and the answers would come to me. I no longer was driving the car; I handed the wheel to *him*. I had surrendered to *his* driving. It sounds insane yet it has been the most powerful experience I have lived.

I'm happy to say that things did change and with every obstacle I remind myself that *he* is in control. That my power, my communication is the result I create and envision with gratitude in advance for what HE is doing in my life. It's called faith. My faith provided me the strength to continue and recognize this too shall pass. That everything I experience leads to something greater. The growth I had at that time was a foundation for more of life. The gift of self-discovery through this process gave me strength to seek more of life. I felt supported, protected and never alone again.

Circumstance does not make the man;
it reveals him to himself.

JAMES ALLEN

TRUST

What did trust mean to me? I was brought up in such a loving family. Going to church was not a ritual but it was a part of our lives. The emotion of trust never was on my forefront. I never thought about it. I possibly came to have some awareness of it as a young child when my parents would say, "Do not trust strangers." Then when a little older, the advice would be "don't trust everyone, including family." Then when a little older still, "don't put all your trust on that boy." Trust turned out to be a necessary foundation for my growth.

I had an understanding to trust God and my parents. No one else qualified. I never questioned what it meant to trust. The idea is so small and yet so powerful. I learned a deeper sense of trust in my marriage and with my kids and yet before this I would have said I was always confident I had a full understanding of the word. I didn't realize there could be so many levels of depth in getting to the true meaning of the word. Yet there is. Trust doesn't belong to others, it's not about if it's convenient or right or wrong, or if its deserved. Trust is based on a higher source that eliminates anything and anyone around you. It's a relationship that has layers of depth that is just unimaginable, it provides peace in my soul. Trust provides me strength through any obstacle and happiness and laughter in receiving great results. It's *present* within me all the time.

My intuition supports my decisions, and my imagination allows expansion. It is that knowing that allows you to stand firm on the ground. Trust is the integrity within you, the letting go of the past, and requires that you be present in the here and now. The now is where imagination is leading you. Trust is that source within you that stirs up questions allowing you to see and acknowledge that something is being communicated to you. It is that voice that we sometimes ignore because we think we know better. It is also the knowing we are always being guided. Trust is the action of that, that you want. Faith is the peace within the action towards its deliverance.

EXPANSION AND HEALING

Expansion and healing are probably the best two words to describe my journey. Six months before my season with my mother I had begun my coaching career, not necessarily knowing why this was placed in my path. I was passionate about personal growth and serving people. I was at the beginning of this new path of growth and expansion.

When my father passed, I had closed a chapter in my life I was no longer passionate about and truly dived into finding my purpose. Life felt different and I didn't feel alive. I was extremely clear that I would not live a life without purpose. I remember thinking if I learned anything from my father, it was not to settle. Even though his experience was different, I knew my father was missing that fire in him. There was a sense of emptiness in his life. There was nothing and no one that could have given him that but himself. I learned from him to live better than he did. To be happier than he was. To pursue what I want and not to settle or do what others tell you should be done. He had a one-track mind.

I dived into coaching, not because I had experience but because it lit my fire! I have come to learn that I can only give what I have to give. I can only serve if I have something to offer. I have learned to place myself first not because I'm more important but because I am not able to give what I don't have. And *yes*, I am more important. Does that make me selfish? Or does *me* expressing that empower you to love yourself more? See most people would think it's selfish because we have this understanding as woman, we are to care for others; therefore, people expect that already from us. But what are they really saying? *Take care of me before you take care of yourself.* And is that not selfish of them? Hmmmm… yes read it again… Did that provide more clarity?

Yes, self-love brings a depth of expansion and healing. My perception shifted because I am now thinking and breathing new beliefs that serve me, that empower me; I can see with different set of eyes. I empower others to see the beauty within themselves. As a daughter, I empower my mother to see things with a different perspective. As a wife and mother of three amazing young adults, I play a big role as they learn to love themselves and know and believe they can pursue dreams bigger than they can imagine. As a coach it is my purpose to serve, to help you discover that quantum leap within yourself. My purpose with this chapter is to ignite your fire. Wherever you are in life, there is always something deeper, more beautiful to discover of yourself and within yourself. The possibilities are endless.

I'm grateful for the unknown determination I found to get answers. I'm grateful for the time I spent with my father; we had so many deep conversations. Not all were happy or wonderful but deep and eye opening they were. Something that I will always carry with me.

The greatest glory in living lies not in never falling,
but in rising every time we fall.

NELSON MANDELA

*Nothing on earth
can break the power
of the human spirit.*

GREG HICKMAN

DELLA WADDELL

Della Waddell is a published author and a certified life coach. Her passion is helping others overcome life's challenges. She is the mother of two young adults and currently lives in Ontario, Canada with her dogs, Bear and Bentley.

AUTHENTIC WARRIOR

DELLA WADDELL

A really strong woman accepts
the war she went through
and is ennobled by her scars.

CARLY SIMON

No one intentionally goes into marriage with the mindset that one day you might end up in divorce. However, when things get ugly, we do wonder how the hell did we get here? Looking back at that naïve twenty-two-year-old me, those vows of *"for better or worse"* were a serious commitment. The adults in my world bestowed upon me their sage advice that marriage is hard work and to never give up. Those words *"for better or worse"* echoed in my head for years and as each anniversary slipped away, those marital challenges became all too real. I found myself often questioning my own happiness. Yet, like many relationships, the longer it is, the greater the chance that large acquired debts and growing family units will solidify the union so that when the honeymoon stage is long gone, what you have created will make you both stronger together. This is what I believed was my life and

I cherished it. When asked where did I find the strength to change, that's when I realized it was not all I thought it was. My answer would seem simple and yet it has taken me a long time to discover.

It's been several painful years since the big day when my marriage went sideways. It has taken me several additional years to find myself again and understand how I managed to come out the other side.

THE FAÇADE

My husband and I had become the proverbial two ships passing in the night. We were *that* family. From the outside, we appeared like a loving, cohesive unit—posting fantastic Instagram-worthy family vacation pictures online, hosting big parties at our beautiful home, and sharing the perfect family Christmas shots on social media. But life inside the bubble was another story altogether. Early on I devoted myself to the role of the housewife with the belief that it was the place I would be the most useful for our household, although, in hindsight, that was a very limited vision of my potential.

My own childhood example was that of a hardworking businessman father who provided for the family while my mom stayed home and raised four children. Although she worked equally as hard as my father, I was always aware that somehow her efforts were not overly valued—yet here I was, following in my mother's footsteps while hoping for a different outcome. Who were we really fooling? Truth was, we weren't a cohesive family unit working together for common goals. My husband and I were leading separate lives; my world was reduced to caring for everyone else but me. My identity boiled down to wife and mother. Although we had agreed I would stay home while he built his business, I often felt conflicted because I felt I had lost myself.

I once had dreams of pursuing a career. This is where my personal conflict started. I did love the time I spent with the children and found myself filled with purpose and pride watching my children grow up and my family take shape. I believed my worth in our family union hinged upon me doing everything possible to please in the hopes that my efforts would be appreciated by those I served. The cycle of a people pleaser was that the less I felt appreciated, the harder I tried to do and be more so that I could be recognized by my husband. Eventually I found myself frustrated and lost, my husband surly and dismissive, my life speeding towards an outcome that I had never contemplated. We barely spoke to one another. He slept with his back to me and I felt invisible. It had become apparent that our marriage was in peril. The more neglect I felt, the harder I worked at trying to salvage the marriage. The only one that had been essentially fooled, was in fact, me.

EYES WIDE OPEN

"Do you love me? I asked. His reply "Define love."

Late one afternoon as I was passing through the hallway, a voice inside prompted me to reach inside his jacket pocket. The tips of my fingers felt the hard shell of his phone. Slowly taking it out my eyes gazed at the screen and there it was. "Hopping in the shower, wish you were here." My hands started shaking with such force that for a second my brain wasn't sure what to do. My heart sank. At that moment, I decided not to say anything. I was devastated.

After confronting him, his denial mixed with being totally blindsided left me angry and confused. For months he was off, and the more I felt pushed into a corner the more I threatened him with divorce. We had even gotten to the point where we decided to purchase a second home to create separate lives but deep down I wanted him to fight for me, so I resisted. I was mad! I was angry that he didn't care about his family and above all that, it was clear he cared very little for me.

Not long after discovering that text message on a cold February morning, I could barely crawl out of bed. My head hurt from lack of sleep. I shuffled to the bathroom and I just stood there looking into the mirror. The woman staring back at me didn't look like me at all, or so I thought. She had black circles around her eyes, hair thinning from stress, she was overweight, and there were tears staining her face. The excruciating hurt was rising to the surface.

Who had I become? Where did I go? My emotions were peaked. Anger, resentment, hurt, sadness, fear, all mixed into one now. It was now or never. There was no fixing this or sweeping it under the rug. The writing was on the wall and he had checked out. My brain couldn't shut off. The enormous betrayal broke my heart. The lies, the deception, the infidelity was now too much for me to deal with and action was needed. I stormed out of that bathroom with such determination that self-doubt and fear were not present at that moment.

I opened the closet doors and I packed what he would need to stay away from our home. My inner strength was my driving force. At that moment my soul needed respect and love; I realized that I deserved it all! My eyes were wide open now. I had been going to bed for months reciting that I deserved more and now I knew it. After all, I gave up a career to help him build a successful business, he golfed while I cared for the kids, he ate at fancy restaurants while we ate macaroni and cheese for dinner. I did this hoping my contributions at home were equally valued by him to his own work outside of it; although I had put up with a lot, the level of infidelity was unacceptable. That night I drove his stuff to him while he played hockey with the "boys." I filled his car with his belongings, slammed the door and locked it, and then proceeded home.

That drive was long and my thoughts raced. What now? I thought. What the hell am I going to do? Reflecting, I did everything by the book. I had supported him and helped create "his success" by staying at home to raise the kids. We had a huge mortgage, a house in constant renovation, two cars, a business starting to thrive. The realization that I was breaking up the family hit hard! Kicking him out meant that I now had no income and I had teenage kids to take care of. Twenty-two years of marriage gone. My self-worth was non-existent and now I'd lose my status as a wife. I thought back to that reflection of that woman in the mirror, that exhausted shell, and overweight from early menopause. On a very bleak and snowy February night in 2014 I kept asking myself how I had become invisible and how the hell at the age of 44 I was going to move on.

PULLED UP MY BIG GIRL PANTS

A couple of weeks later my life as a newly separated woman began to unfold even if I didn't want it to. It dawned on me now more than ever that this separation was never about him. In all honesty, I was lonelier in my marriage than I had yet to feel. I was shocked at this epiphany.

I realized that life wanted me to change lanes and shake things up, for me. Settling into the idea of all of the changes was challenging to me. Most days and nights involved crying and so I began to write. It was cathartic to express all of these emotions that I couldn't talk to anyone about. I wrote about my sadness, the loss of my partner, the lonely bed, and my feelings that I was middle-aged with nothing to offer. I smiled when the kids came to check on me and the tears resumed when the door closed. I lived like this for months, completely sinking in my own thoughts and despair.

After crying enough to drown in my own tears, I saw that the days had moved into weeks and then months. I started to feel stronger and I had *that* moment: as I liked to say, it was time to "pull up my big girl pants." I forced myself to get dressed each day, to look respectable and get organized. This was the hardest time of my life. I constantly questioned myself, "Who *am* I?"

Three months after we separated, I had lost thirty pounds intentionally, and started to like my new shape. Physically, I was learning to really love myself; however, emotionally, I was still a mess. Every single day I set out to "pick myself up," and I did although it was incredibly difficult. It was truly a conscious and continuous effort.

GO AHEAD AND GET DATING

To say that the first year of being separated was a blur is an understatement. I would constantly re-evaluate my entire life. I hung onto things from the past, replayed scenarios over again in my head but externally showed a poker face, like all was great and I didn't have any cares in the world.

One day my sister said "ok, it's time for you to start dating." My face went pale with terror. *Dating? OMG.* I had never even thought about seriously getting out there. I was aghast when she told me she was sick of seeing me mope around. She sat down beside me and filled out the initial information on an online dating site, then passed the laptop to me when the prompt on the screen said, "Go Ahead and Get Dating." I sat there frozen.

There were so many questions to answer to get started, it was overwhelming. I must have stared at that page for days and constantly called my friends to validate each of my answers. "Do I like sightseeing in the city or am I more a "hikes in the country" type of girl?" They all laughed and told me to get on with it. I kept at it and reviewed my draft profile. I hesitantly clicked on "accept" and my profile popped up. The world of dating began. I hadn't been on a date in over twenty-three years, and it was "old school," actually meeting people in person first. Now I was in my forties and had kids and life experience. I was scared shitless.

The first three months was a total introduction to "the world" out there. The faces of potential dates, their stories, their likes/dislikes. Some were arrogant, some funny, from all different walks of life. Some men tall, some short, bald ones, fat ones, even fake ones, it was insane. My cell phone constantly flashed as notifications alerted me that someone had looked at my profile, or when there was a new message, and even when there was a new profile for me to consider. Online dating occupied me like it was my job! I started to feel like a small-town version of *Sex and the City*, flipping between feeling introverted and shy like Charlotte and feeling empowered and bold like Carrie.

My late nights consisted of sitting in bed, still in my pj's with a spoon fresh out of the ice cream container with my eyes glued to the screen staring at countless profile pictures of men holding fish. My mind was perplexed about what the message was that they were trying to send: Is this a caveman concept? Me man, you woman, I hunt, you cook? I giggled aloud at the thought and this surprised me as it reminded me how little I had laughed in the last years of my marriage. All of sudden I felt alive and validated through my new experiences. I scooped another spoonful of ice cream in my mouth and kept scrolling.

The message from one man attracted my attention. His message was direct but accurate: *"Online dating is a place for people who are recently coming out of situations to find validation from others of who they are. The ones that have been on here a long time just keep recycling and haven't learned anything. What have you learned?"* My first instinct was to ignore him, my easy go-to reaction when confronted. Funny how something can trigger you and he did. After twenty-four hours I responded, expressing that his note was interesting and I thanked him for his message. I then continued on with my life lessons. He wrote me back, however, I didn't pursue any further interaction. It was at that time, my eyes opened. I realized that all of these people were and are and are looking for the same thing. *Love.* To me, it seems that kindness was key.

Three months passed and definitely "matched" out, my subscription was ending, thousands of views, hundreds of emails hoping to entice me, and yet I'd sent only a few back. You see, at this age it became apparent to me that we all have some "baggage" and when a man wrote he wanted to meet someone without baggage, I questioned that. We all were once, maybe twice married, some with small kids, no kids, older kids, and had lost someone who had been special to us through divorce or death. We all bring *stuff* to the table. What was more important to me was someone who had learned about themselves and how they got here. In hindsight, this actually took me a few years to understand. In the meanwhile, I still continued to thank people, extend a kind word of acknowledgment of appreciation, as my heart knew how lonely life could be. During this process, I started to grow and understand myself. I think that we all have expectations of what is a fit for us. Looking back, I used to say I didn't have expectations from others yet as time went by it became apparent that I did. Honesty is one characteristic I own.

While my online dating membership was coming to a close, I did manage to go on many coffee dates. Online dating can be challenging until after you meet. Expectations about bodies because phone app filters might have been used sure got to me. The few people I met said I was exactly as I appeared online. Over the next couple of years, I did go back online to different sites and met some wonderful men and even had a few short relationships but I still needed time to heal. Not all of my dating experiences were bad but some were definitely giggle-worthy.

FEEDING MY SOUL

The years have passed and it has been quite a journey of the soul. I went back to school for fashion design, thinking it was my passion until the details of the course made it clear that it wasn't. Then I went into making bath bombs for a soap store, then I took an online course in hypnotherapy, but all the while the one thing that was consistent was my writing. Each day I wrote about my everyday achievements. I believed that my world was expanding and I met people everywhere.

Soon everything started to inspire me. Music filled my house again, I began to write more and the more inspired I was, the more I shared my story. I stopped living under the shadow of someone else, moved out of my environment, and I learned how to deal with my anxiety, forcing myself to keep moving. I constantly stepped out of my comfort zone in my dating life and everything else I chose to surround myself with. I have made mistakes, said one thing and done another. I have confused my friends and family around me with my decision to stay kind to my ex-husband but again it's my story, and I am not apologizing for any behavior that feeds my soul and is true to me. I learned to embrace a level of kindness while navigating all levels of self-awareness. Would I advise anyone else to do what I did? Well, it wouldn't be up to me to tell them that. They, need to figure it out for themselves, as I did.

Still, it seemed to take me longer to do what others seem to do so easily. This made me wonder if there was something wrong with me. Too picky, too afraid, too damaged—what was it? I learned that I simply needed to understand myself to set myself free. To forgive my ex, to forgive myself, to love myself, to learn to listen and to breathe. I realized that my need to forgive was my perception. And although it had been years since our initial separation, it had not settled so I needed more time than others. I saw that my feelings of shame, guilt, and embarrassment diminished as the time passed. My own self-awareness, values, and voice were coming back. With nothing further to lose, communication with my ex-husband became more honest and although old emotions came to the surface occasionally, we became more considerate about working out the business of co-parenting our children causing a level of kindness between us to blossom. Although unsuccessful as a couple, our parenting skills evolved in a way that allowed our children to see the good examples of how adversity can help you come out even better than before. Time allowed all of us to heal and things became more amicable.

It was hard, but facing the truth, learning important lessons, never giving up, going back to school, finding my value, and feeling appreciated allowed me to become internally peaceful to the point that now gratitude was present. Separation and divorce is hard on everyone. Emotions are high but time does heal. Communication is so important for healing and we just kept approaching each other with kindness. This was not usual for us during our marriage so I was surprised that we kept it up as I never saw this continuing on. It is a unique relationship to say the least.

Life has no guarantees as we know. For the past few years, issues with my health came to the forefront. Some people believe that when we go for years without acknowledging the mental and spiritual balance of our bodies, it will eventually affect us emotionally, spiritually, and physically. I cannot say this is what caused my health issues but I had to deal with them regardless. I underwent two unexpected surgeries to remove major organs and skin cancer, yet I did not stop. This propelled me into achieving my coaching certificate in the middle of the COVID-19 pandemic lockdown, while lying in bed recovering from my surgeries.

I have learned to take responsibility for my part in the relationships I have with both family and friends as well as the good parts and the breakdown of my marriage. Looking into myself, I have seen my transformation into the person I am and I feel empowered. With all the dating experiences, truth is, in the end, the most beautiful thing is that I actually chose myself. The lesson is you have to love yourself first. That can take time for many people as we have to learn to love and accept ourselves. Happiness is something internal not external. For all those women in my life that continue to inspire me constantly, it's my turn to help others that need to find their purpose and happiness. Coaching is my way of giving back and I see that my journey has led me to this as my soul purpose.

My once perfected façade, my "insta ready" poker face, is long gone. I have embraced my beautiful scars and show them on the outside. These are my battle wounds and honestly, I am more than okay with that as these have led me to where I am today, which is where I am supposed to be. I now live genuinely and openly as my authentic self. I live in my power and know that with every challenge I will face in the future, I will overcome as I am a warrior. My journey has given me the gift to understand that I will never underestimate myself in any capacity again.

As I look back on my journey starting with my separation which sparked my metamorphosis all those years ago, I realize that I have always chosen myself. Sure, I could have stayed with my ex-husband and lived within that illusion of happiness and pretended that his indiscretion didn't exist in exchange for comfort and living that status quo. When challenged, which was really a first for me, my gut reaction was to be true to myself even though I didn't really know what that even meant. I only knew how it felt. Again, throughout the dating process, it was really about the journey to finding myself, who I was, who I am, and where I was going. It hasn't been about finding someone to be co-dependent on, but rather two whole people that come together, if that happens. I am now constantly stepping out of my comfort zone, kicking my fear to the side because I have the mindset that if it calls out to my soul, it will help me grow into the woman I am becoming.

The most powerful relationship you will ever have is the relationship with yourself.

STEVE MARABOLI

ACKNOWLEDGMENTS

LISA ANDERSON

I would like to dedicate my story to my husband Frank and to my son Joshua for all their support. I could not be more proud of our family of three and of course little Libby my dog and co-pilot.

NATASHA AZADI

I would like thank those that have stood by my side through my ongoing journey, through the highs and lows.

Special gratitude goes to my step mum Sharon, special friends Kelly and Debra without your support and guidance this would have not been possible.

RANJINI CASSUP

Gratitude to everyone who challenged me to do more, be more, live more. Thank you to my friends who never judged me, my children who always loved me, my husband for allowing me the space and time I needed for self-reflection and growth. I love you endlessly.

ACKNOWLEDGMENTS

JENNIFER CHAPMAN

First and foremost, I'd like to thank my husband Ray for his unwavering love and support through my recovery and now my new business.

Second, my entire family for always being by my side and cheering me on every step of the way.

My friends, my coworkers past and present, my medical team and therapists for pushing me to be one step better every single day.

PATRICIA DE PICCIOTTO

Thank you Mom for inspiring and guiding me on this journey. You raised me with your loving presence and I will continue growing with your absence.

Patrick, Edward, Raphael and Benjamin your love and support are my rock every day.

To my father and sisters, I know you are with me, even an ocean apart.

HEATHER DI SANTO

To Dad and Nana, whose guidance from above inspired this chapter of my story. For my mom, whose tenacity I admire and will serve me well in the next phase of my journey. Love to my husband and boys who are the light of my world.

BRI DIMIT

Thank you, Carol Starr Taylor and Star House Publishing, for your aid while writing this chapter. Immense gratitude goes towards my husband Jordan, my outstanding community, and my mom for their wisdom, advocacy, and love. Finally, I'd like to thank myself for having the courage, vulnerability, and grit to share my story.

ERIN MONTGOMERY

I want to dedicate this chapter to my mom and sisters, who have always been there for me. We have faced some rocky paths together but we also seem to come out the other side. I also want to dedicate this chapter to my angel in heaven. You have taught me so much and I know you are always watching over me.

CASSANDRA NAGEL

I cannot express enough gratitude to my phenomenal husband Jason, my children Tristan and Catrina for encouraging me to continue writing. I love you all big-big like the sky.

To everyone in my life past-or-present, to my three soul-sisters; you know who you are, I send my gratitude and love.

FRANCA NAVARRA

To my sons Christopher, Andrew, Matthew and Liam. Thank you for loving me as your Mama, and for being my reasons to heal and evolve into the survivor I am today. You all have been my greatest teachers. Christopher you have taught me patience. Andrew you have taught me determination. Matthew you taught me to stay positive. And Liam you have taught me to live in hope. I love you all.

ACKNOWLEDGMENTS

CARL RICHARDS

To my husband Jeff for his love and support... and for walking life's journey together.

To my parents John and Jeannine, brothers, Paul and Gordon and the rest of my family for support and accepting both Jeff and I.

To my friends and colleagues, too many to mention!

To Carol Starr Taylor for helping me tell the full story.

REESHEMAH STIDHUM

To my dearest Tawnya, you said I could write a book about my adversities as we reminisced and laughed about those turbulent times. Your physical spirit taught me what *true* friendship embodies. You're indeed irreplaceable. I'm honored our paths crossed in this lifetime and know our souls will meet again.

MARSHA MYLES TERRY

Thank you, God, for the courage to share my journey. Thank you to my mentors and coaches who believed in me. Thank you to my family who has always supported me in everything I do. Most of all thank you to my biggest cheerleader my husband, Onuwa. I love you.

MARIEKE VAN ASTEN

Through all the ups and downs in my life, my parents always supported me, no matter what. I am forever grateful to them.

A big thank you to my family and friends who continue to support me in my journey to make the Breadfruit House Dominica Foundation a success.

KAREM ZAFRA-VERA

Daddy, my words are dedicated to you.

To Victoria, Izabella and Christopher you ignite my light to be more because you see more of me.

To Micani, thank you for your support and love, always unshakable. I love you.

Troy, thank you for always showing up when you didn't have to.

DELLA WADDELL

Thank you to my mom, sisters Daye and Linda for their incredible support.

To Tanya, Krista and Karen, I am hugely indebted to you all.

To my children Cassidy and Christian you made me strong, you made me laugh, you gave me hope and that is more than I could have ever imagined.

CPSIA information can be obtained
at www.ICGtesting.com
Printed in the USA
BVHW041800021121
620550BV00007B/396